Heather Driscoll

Yorks...
Mour... ...iking
The North Dales

VERTEBRATE **GRAPHICS**
PUBLISHING

Design and production by Vertebrate Graphics Ltd, Sheffield
www.**v-graphics**.co.uk

Green Lanes

A non-legal term for an unsurfaced country road. There is some debate as to who's allowed to use them, but right now, cyclists are OK.

White Roads

White roads have no recorded status. They often appear to be farm tracks or private roads when they are actually public highways. There are an estimated 7000km of 'lost' white roads around the UK and many are great, totally legal trails. (You need to check the definitive map at your local highway authority to be absolutely sure – if in doubt stick to a bridleway.) **If you're not familiar with the symbols denoting bridleways, footpaths and so on, check the information section on your map.**

Not all tracks are signed. What this means is that it's not always obvious whether that great-looking trail you want to follow is an illegal footpath or a legal bridleway. That's why it's a good idea to carry a map with you on every ride. Here are some suggestions why it's a good idea to stick to legit trails:

1   Not doing so annoys the people we need to impress if we're ever going to have more (legal) two-wheeled access to the countryside.
2   Technically speaking, you're trespassing if you ride on a footpath – no matter how wide – and you could be prosecuted by the landowner for any damage caused
3   Riding on footpaths can upset walkers, who have every right to enjoy their day.
4   Sticking to rights of way helps preserve fragile moorland habitats, whereas bashing through overgrown greenery will play havoc with your shifting.

The bike

Any half-decent mountain bike will be fine (although you're probably better off avoiding a "£99 special"). A full suspension bike will add comfort and control. A lightweight race number will make hills easier and something with a bit of travel will help on technical descents. Ideally, we'd pick the best compromise between all three, which is probably what you already have.

Check everything's working – you won't be going uphill fast if your gears seize but you'll be a little faster than planned if your brakes don't work. Pump the tyres up, check nothing's about to wear through and make sure that everything that should be tight is tight. If you can't do this yourself, visit your local bike shop.

As ever, these grades are subjective. How you find a particular route, downhill or climb will be dictated by your own levels of fitness and skill (or bottle).

Maps, descriptions, distances

While every effort has been made to ensure accuracy within the maps and descriptions in this guide, things change from time to time and we are unable to guarantee that every detail will be correct.

Note that distances have been measured from the map and may not tally with a bike computer. Treat stated distances as a guideline only.

Rights of way

To the best of our knowledge, all of the routes in this guide are totally legal and mountain bikers have what is termed 'Right of Way'. (This doesn't mean that you actually have the right of way – you don't – just that you are allowed to be there.)

Rights of way include

Footpaths (yellow arrows)

Usually the most tempting trails around, but off-limits to mountain bikers. Please don't ride them – you've no right to be there, will upset, and possibly endanger other users and won't do our reputation any good at all.

Bridleways (blue arrows)

Go for it! Bear in mind that you'll be sharing the trails with walkers and horses.

Byways Open to All Traffic (red arrows)

Otherwise known as BOATs, these allow all traffic access, including vehicles – although, surprisingly, we've yet to see a boat on a BOAT. This means that you may well be sharing the trail with motorcyclists and 4×4 enthusiasts – often to be seen enjoying the peace, quiet and fresh air of the countryside.

Forestry Commission Land

Officially, you need permission to ride on FC land. However, this has often been granted, and the FC generally regards cycling favourably. A note of caution: beware of forestry operations – a fully loaded logging truck could easily scuff your paintwork!

Acknowledgements

Thanks to Mark Allum of the Yorkshire Dales National Park Authority for his support with the project, and the YDNPA itself for the great work it has done restoring many previously unrideable bridleways.

Andy Heading, for his excellent photography, input, suggestions and bike-dodging.

The VG team – Nathan Ryder and Oliver Jackson for their excellent design work, Tom Fenton for his editing and Jon Barton and Simon Norris for backing the projects and their work on earlier volumes which paved the way for this one.

Susan Harvey at Harvey Maps, for her help in providing mapping data.

Karen McDonald at Polaris for providing clothing for our photo sessions.

And to our photographic models, Andrew Whittaker, Ben Eagle, Pete Dodd, Rosemary Lakin and Freya Bloor, for putting up with Andy's endless requests to "ride up that hill again".

How to use this book

The routes

We've tried to cover as many of the North Dales' numerous trails as possible in this guide, whilst avoiding bog trotting, seeking out the more 'interesting' sections and taking in the bits that everybody should ride at some point. The routes we've come up with are just some of the vast number of ways of doing this. Try them as suggested, in reverse or joined to neighbouring routes. Once you've ridden a few and got to know the area a little, you'll be able to link your favourite trails into nice flowing rides where you don't need a map or guidebook at all.

Classics are generally fairly short (although not necessarily easy). **Epics** are a little longer and climb a little more. **Enduros** are a step up again, and the **Killer Loops** are self-explanatory. We've also listed our pick of the area's descents and climbs, which may help you choose you route.

Grades

We've graded the routes (and key climbs and descents) as Blue, Red or Black, in a similar system to that being adopted on several of the man-made trails around the UK.

▲ = Medium, ▲ = Hard and ▲ = Extreme.

These grades are based on summer conditions – little or no mud and dry Dales limestone. In a drought they may feel easier, in the depths of winter, harder. They take into account technicality, length and remoteness. So one 'black' route might be a short techno fest whilst another could be a big endurance challenge.

Introduction

The Dales offer an excellent network of stone-based bridleways, awesome scenery rising above 700m and, because of the spread-out nature of the trails, very little conflict with other users. In fact, they're mountain biking heaven on excellent trails weaving through a landscape of limestone plateaux, drystone walls, field barns, pasture, broadleaf woodland, streams, rivers and waterfalls with fine pubs in almost all the villages down through Arkengarthdale (what a name!), Swaledale and Wensleydale. One of the rides here visits the highest pub in England at Tan Hill with a long tough section on the Pennine Way to follow.

Among an enormous list of highlights are the eye-popping descent from the top of the Howgills, the long grassy plateau of Lady Ann Clifford's Highway to the northwest of Hawes, the fast, straight descent along Cam High Road, the atmospheric ruins of the old lead mining industry in Swaledale, like ghost towns left abandoned, and long charges across the heather moors on grouse shooting tracks between Langthwaite and Marske.

There is little singletrack in the Dales as most of the trails either follow broad stone tracks lower down or broad grassy tracks higher up. The more 'interesting' trails in the region do not consist of a series of perfectly spaced drop-offs twisting through woodland but lung-busting 250m climbs up steep stone tracks and loose stone descents where picking the right line has you crossing left to right across the path dodging the rubble traps.

The icing on the cake consists of long cruising plateau sections on well-drained grass, normally coming as a reward for some horrendous climb and offering you the chance to sniff the breeze and open your eyes to the stupendous scenery that lies all around, before the gradient steepens and you need to sharpen your wits for the downhill challenges.

Good bases in the north Dales with a fine selection of pubs, cafes and accommodation include Reeth, with access to the trails in Swaledale and Arkengarthdale; Bainbridge, Askrigg or Hawes for the trails in Wensleydale and Langstrothdale; and Sedbergh for the Howgills and Dentdale.

Nick Cotton

KEY TO THE MAP SYMBOLS

S **AS**	Starting point, alternative starting point
	Short cut, optional route
2	Waypoint
⊙⊙►	Link to another route
▲ ⋀	Medium ascent, descent
▲ ⋀	Hard ascent, descent
▲ ⋀	Very hard ascent, descent
🍺 ☕	Public house, café
PO ○	Post office, viewpoint
Y **V**	Youth hostel, visitor centre
P ☎	Car park, payphone
🚐 🚐	Caravan site, caravan & campsite
✕ 🗼	Campsite, aerial or mast

════════	Dual carriageway
════════	Main road
════════	Wide minor road
════════	Minor road
════════	Residential road
—•—→ ←—	Railway, station, tunnel
- - - - -	Dismantled railway
– – – –	Track or forest road
- - - - -	Path or old track
— - - —	Intermittent path
▪️▫️	Building, settlement, church
□ ⊔ ⌐ ° ○	Ruin, sheepfold
├──┼──┤	Powerline

The representation of a road, track or footpath is no evidence of the existence of a right of way

RIGHTS OF WAY The information on public rights of way is given in good faith, but is not necessarily an accurate record of legal status. Liability is disclaimed for any inaccuracies. Please check with the relevant local authority for the latest amendments.

•••••••	**Public footpath:** with path on the ground,
- - - - -	without path on the ground
⌐⌐⌐⌐	**Public bridleway:** with path on the ground
○ ○ ○ ○ ○	without path on the ground
- - - - -	**Permissive path** (permission may be withdrawn)
–⋅–⋅–⋅	**Long distance path**

SCALE: 1 grid square equals 1 kilometre

	Lake, jetty, island
	Small lake, pond
	River, footbridge
	Wide stream
	Narrow stream
	Peat hags
	Marshy ground
	Farmland
	Fell or moorland
	Open forest or woodland
	Dense plantation
	Forest ride or firebreak
	Boundary maintained
	Boundary remains

On moorland, walls and fences are shown.
For farmland, only the outer boundary wall or fence is shown.

	Contour (15m interval)
	Index contour (75m interval)
	Cave or mine, auxiliary contour
505	Spot height (in metres – from air survey)
	Predominantly rocky ground
	Major crag, climbing crag
	Spoil heap, sink holes: large, small
	O.S. trig pillar, large cairn
	Pot hole (some dangerous shafts)
	Shaft, large boulder, old workings

Contours change from brown to grey where the ground is predominantly rocky outcrops, small crags and other bare rock.

	900m+
	825–900m
	750–825m
	675–750m
	600–675m
	450–600m
	300–450m
	150–300m
	0–150m

ABBREVIATIONS USED IN ROUTE DIRECTIONS

L = Left   **R** = Right

SA = Straight ahead

Contents

ROUTE GRADES ▲ = MEDIUM ▲ = HARD ▲ = EXTREME (see page viii)

Yorkshire Dales
MountainBiking
The North Dales

VG Copyright © 2006 Vertebrate Graphics Ltd

VG Published by Vertebrate Graphics Ltd

ISBN 0-9548131-5-4

Cover photo: Andy Heading

Photography by Andy Heading
Additional photography Nick Cotton

Design by Nathan Ryder – Vertebrate Graphics Ltd.
Production by Oliver Jackson – Vertebrate Graphics Ltd.
Series editor Tom Fenton – Vertebrate Graphics Ltd.
www.**v-graphics**.co.uk/publications

Yorkshire Dales
MountainBiking
The North Dales

Written by
Nick Cotton

Photography by **Andy Heading**

What tyres for... ?

In winter you might feel a mud tyre essential, whilst in the dry, few would deny that a fast tyre is more fun. A few routes tackle rocky terrain, so something with a bit of size will help as far as comfort and puncture prevention go. We use all-rounders most of the time.

Essential kit

Helmet

"The best helmet is the one that you're wearing". Just make sure that it fits, that you're wearing it correctly and that it won't move around in a crash.

Clothing

The tried and tested layering system utilising wicking fabrics (not cotton) works really well. Mountain biking is a very active sport, so set off a little on the cool side as you'll soon warm up. Padded shorts are definitely more comfortable, but the amount of lycra on display is down to you.

Don't leave all those essential warm layers behind – you'll be thankful for them on the descents, during snack breaks and if anything goes awry.

Gloves

Gloves help prevent blisters and numb hands and keep your fingers warm in the winter. They also provide a surprising amount of protection when you come off.

Footwear

Flat pedals/SPDs – your call. They aren't going to grip on wet Dales limestone, so don't worry about that, but make sure they have sufficient tread for everywhere else. Consider overshoes if it's chilly.

Other Essentials

As mentioned, take any necessary spares, tools, tube and pump, spare clothes, first aid kit, food and water. Stop short of the kitchen sink, as you'll still want to be able to actually ride your bike.

You'll need something to carry this little lot in. We'd suggest a hydration pack, as they allow you to drink on the move and keep excess weight off the bike.

Maps

Harvey Maps:
- Yorkshire Dales North
- Yorkshire Dales South
- Yorkshire Dales East
- Yorkshire Dales West

Ordnance Survey:
- OL19 Howgill Fells & Upper Eden Valley
- OL30 Yorkshire Dales: Northern and Central Areas
- OL2 Yorkshire Dales: Southern & Western areas

Night riding

Night riding opens up a whole new world of fun. It's possible to enjoy an after-work ride in the depths of winter in your favourite off-road playground. Night riding is ace, but it's a completely different ball game and (hardly surprisingly) there are a few risks to be aware of.

PHOTO COURTESY OF LUMICYCLE

Lights and batteries

Invest carefully in a lighting system. We've been using the excellent **Lumicycle** range. Consider battery life, weight, number/ type of bulbs and power. Ensure that your battery is fully charged before you ride (sounds like common sense, but we've done it!). Carry a secondary light source (such as a head torch) for emergencies (it's surprising what you can ride with a commuter light if you have to, although it isn't much fun). Ensure that you pack a rear light for road sections and keep it clean.

Route planning and safety

Choose your ride on the basis of battery life. (Time it yourself, don't necessarily rely on the manufacturer's information.) Allow extra time – you'll probably be slower in the dark. Stay on ground that you are familiar with at first (night-time navigation in unfamiliar territory demands military expertise) and not too far from home. Ride with a friend. Watch out for the werewolves. Tell someone you're out. **Ride within your limits – trees loom up very quickly in the dark!**

General safety (a.k.a. 'commonsense')

Many of the routes described are challenging and point you at tough climbs and steep descents, which can potentially be very dangerous. Too much exuberance on a slippery descent in the middle of nowhere and you could be in more than a spot of bother, especially if you're alone. Consider your limitations and relative fragility before launching at something.

Be self-sufficient. Carry plenty of food and water, spares, tube and pump. Consider a first-aid kit. Even if it's warm, the weather could turn, so take a wind/waterproof. Think about what could happen on an enforced stop. Pack lights if you might finish in the dark.

The ability to read a map, navigate in poor visibility and to understand weather warnings is essential. Don't head out in bad weather, unless you're confident and capable.

If you're riding solo, think about the potential seriousness of an accident – you could be without help for a considerable length of time. Tell someone where you are going and when to expect you back. Take a phone if you have one, but don't rely on getting a signal. (And don't call out mountain rescue because you've grazed you knee.)

Riding in a group is safer (ambitious overtaking manoeuvres excepted) and usually more fun, but don't leave the slower members of your party behind and give them a minute for a breather when they've caught up. Allow extra time for a group ride, as you'll inevitably be dealing with punctures or mechanicals.

As the area is popular, ride in control. Bells might be annoying, but they work. If you can't bring yourself to bolt one on, a polite 'excuse me' should be fine.

On hot, sunny days, slap on the Factor 30+ and **always wear your helmet!**

Rules of the (off) road

1   Always ride on legal trails.
2   Ride considerately – give way to horses and pedestrians.
3   Don't spook animals.
4   Ride in control – you don't know who's around the next corner.
5   Leave gates as you find them – if you're unsure, shut them.
6   Keep the noise down and don't swear loudly when you fall off in front of walkers.
7   Leave no trace – take home everything you took out.
8   Keep water sources clean – don't take toilet stops near streams.
9   Enjoy the countryside and respect its life and work.

Thanks to:

Planning your ride

This book should provide you with all the information you need for a good ride. The following tips might also of help:

- Choose your route. Consider the ability/ experience of each rider in your group. Check the weather forecast. How much time do you have available?
- Study the route description carefully before setting off. Cross-reference this the relevant map so that you've got a good sense of general orientation in case you need an escape route.
- Bear in mind all we've suggested about safety, clothing, spares and food and drink.

Get out there and get dirty!

Mountain rescue
In the event of an accident requiring mountain rescue assistance:
Dial 999 and ask for POLICE – MOUNTAIN RESCUE

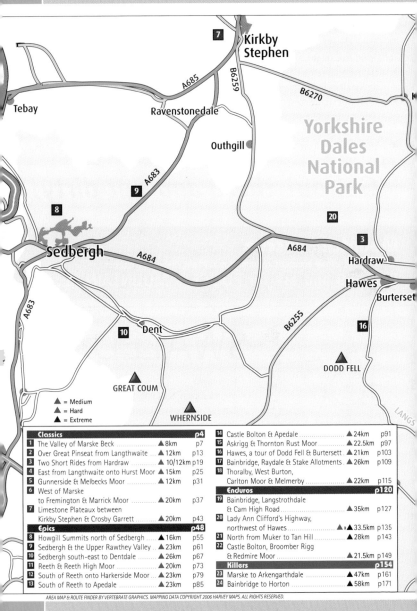

Map legend:

▲ = Medium
▲ = Hard
▲ = Extreme

Kirkby Stephen, Tebay, Ravenstonedale, Outhgill, Yorkshire Dales National Park, Sedbergh, Dent, Hardraw, Hawes, Burtersett, GREAT COUM, WHERNSIDE, DODD FELL

A685, B6259, B6270, A683, A684, B6255

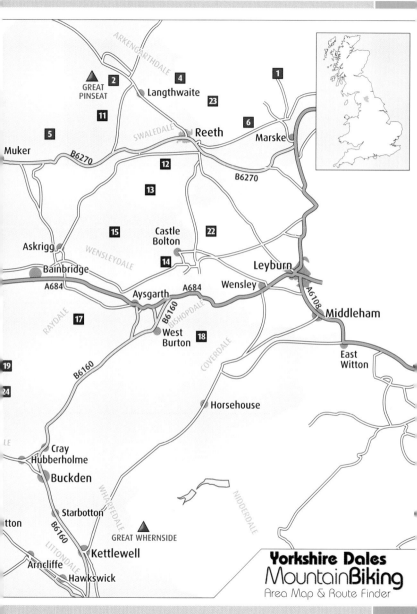

GREAT PINSEAT

Langthwaite

2

4

11

23

1

6

Marske

Reeth

5

Muker

B6270

SWALEDALE

ARKENGARTHDALE

12

B6270

13

15

WENSLEYDALE

Castle Bolton

22

Askrigg

Bainbridge

14

Leyburn

A684

Wensley

A684

Aysgarth

B6160

BISHOPDALE

RAYDALE

A6108

Middleham

17

West Burton

18

COVERDALE

East Witton

19

B6160

24

Horsehouse

NIDDERDALE

Cray
Hubberholme

Buckden

WHARFEDALE

Starbotton

tton

B6160

GREAT WHERNSIDE

LITTONDALE

Kettlewell

Arncliffe

Hawkswick

Yorkshire Dales
Mountain**Biking**
Area Map & Route Finder

SECTION 1

Classics

A quick blast after work, a night loop you can finish before your lights run dry, or a ride to squeeze in when you're short of time. That's a classic. Relatively low on distance and never taking you too far from the start, these are still good, solid rides.

Short, but not necessarily easy.

Classics
sponsored by **bike**magic.com

www.bikemagic.com

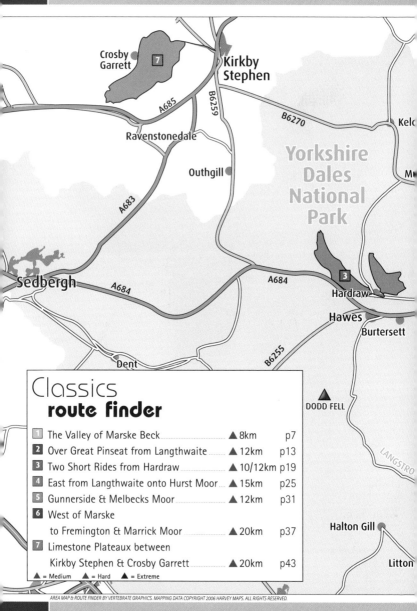

Classics
route finder

▲ = Medium   ▲ = Hard   ▲ = Extreme

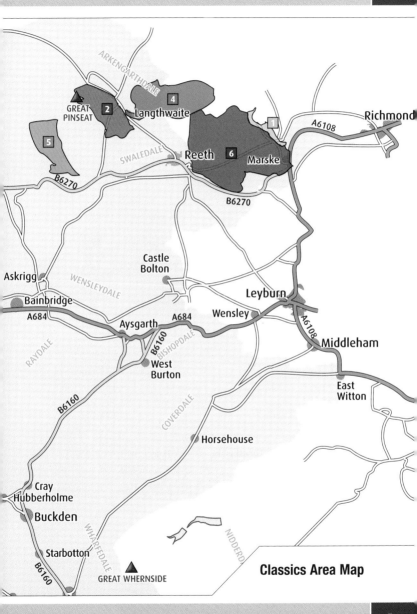

Classics Area Map

CLIMBING OUT OF THE VALLEY

The Valley of **Marske Beck**

Introduction

For much of its life, from first research through to the final stages of writing, this ride has been known as *Marske Smallbut*. Nothing to do with the size of its backside – it is short for *A Small but Perfectly Formed Ride from Marske*. It is like a canapé, an *hors d'oeuvre* before a main meal but thoroughly satisfying for all that. Tough climbs, great views, fine descent, grassy bits, woodland bits, fine old houses.

The Ride

There's a hidden, undiscovered feel about the valley formed by Marske Beck, as though it was made then forgotten about. No less beautiful for that. Climb on road up Skelton Lane then test yourself on how much of the steep stone track you can ride taking you up the hillside to a smooth grass paradise. Drop down into the valley by Telfit Farm, climb again up towards Orgate Farm then glide down through woodland and hidden old houses back to Marske. Enjoy that? Try it in reverse.

Warning: *There are two obvious bridleways nearby that look worth exploring, neither of which gives much joy:*

1 *East towards Richmond there is a dispute about the bridleway through Applegarth and there are several tall stone stiles with narrow gaps in walls making progress by bike very difficult.*
2 *North beyond Orgate Farm (GR 092 019) the bridleway peters out to nothing soon after reaching the top of the hillside.*

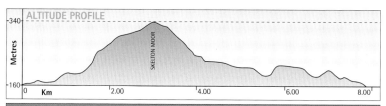

ALTITUDE PROFILE

340

Metres

SKELTON MOOR

160

0   Km   2.00   4.00   6.00   8.00

THE VALLEY OF MARSKE BECK   **GRADE:** ▲

DISTANCE: 8KM

START/FINISH: MARSKE, WEST OF RICHMOND

PARKING: IN MARSKE, JUST WEST OF THE RIVER BRIDGE

PUBLIC HOUSE: THE CLOSEST REFRESHMENTS ARE IN REETH OR RICHMOND

TOTAL ASCENT: 277M

GRID REFERENCE: 104 004

CAFÉ: BRING SANDWICHES

PHOTO: NICK COTTON

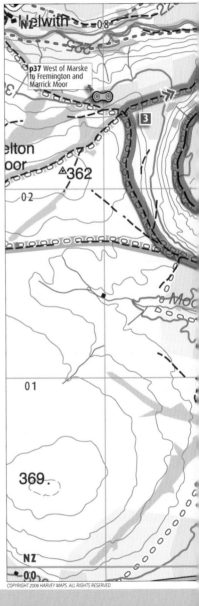

p37 West of Marske to Fremington and Marrick Moor

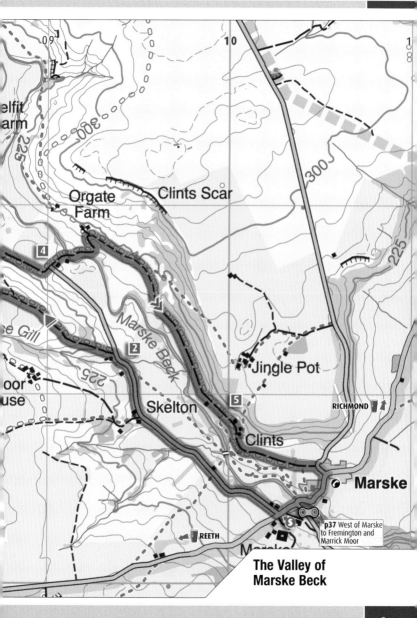

The Valley of
Marske Beck

Directions – The Valley of Marske Beck

⑤► From the car parking area in Marske (GR 104 004) follow the road southwest towards Marrick, Hurst and Reeth. Shortly turn first **R** onto a no through road.

2 After 1.5km, not long after passing the attractive buildings of Skelton Farm, and immediately after Forester's Cottage (both on the left), turn **L** uphill on a wide stone track.

3 Steep climb. At the end of the stone section go through a gate onto a grassy track. **Easy to miss:** 300m after the highpoint, as the descent steepens on a left-hand bend, with a wide grassy track joining from the left, turn sharp **R** downhill on a faint grassy track towards a gate set into the junction of walls (GR 082 024). Follow the track parallel with the wall then zig zag down towards Telfit Farm and turn **R**.

4 After 1.3km at the start of tarmac near the barn, on a sharp right-hand bend, bear **L** downhill (GR 090 017). Cross the bridge over Marske Beck, climb to the top, and with the house (Orgate Farm) to the left, turn **R** onto a wide, firm, grassy track.

5 Enter Clints Wood then at a T-junction with a broad stone track in the woodland bear **R**. Go past houses. At the road junction bear **R** downhill signposted *Richmond* and shortly **R** again downhill to return to the parking area at the start.

◄⚙ Making a day of it

Another ride starts from *Marske* heading west towards *Fremington* – *see page 37*.

YOU'LL PULL FACES LIKE THAT TOO!

Over **Great Pinseat** from **Langthwaite**

12km

Introduction

In this part of the National Park, you are up close to the border with County Durham; it is a very sparsely populated area, remote and very much at the edge, a long way from the popular Dales centres of Wensleydale and Wharfedale. Several tracks lead west from the Tan Hill road but unfortunately in many cases the early promise of fine stone tracks peters out and there is no network of solid stone tracks linking Langthwaite with Tan Hill and Old Gang mines. So this short ride is the best of the rest and certainly has some very testing climbs and roof-the-world cruising. For such a small village, Langthwaite also boasts two pubs – does this have anything to do with its proximity to the hamlet of Booze?

The Ride

Stretch your legs on the lane heading up to Tan Hill before turning off-road towards the mining spoils on Whaw Moor. Just by a round roofed barn there is a fine looking track on the right - this is one of those that starts full of promise only to stop abruptly leaving pushing as the only option. You've bought the book, let me do the grunt work! Back to the ride: climbing over 200m, zig zag up the face of the hillside above the spoil heap, at times steeply, to arrive at the plateau. Turn left and the track gets better and better as you glide through a sea of purple heather with wooded Arkengarthdale down to the left and the path stretching into the distance. A quick shimmy on the lane takes you back off-road for the final grassy descent and return to Langthwaite.

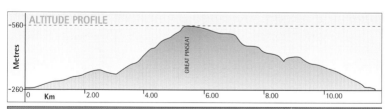

OVER GREAT PINSEAT FROM LANGTHWAITE **GRADE:** ▲

DISTANCE: 12KM

START/FINISH: LANGTHWAITE, NORTHWEST OF REETH

PARKING: PAY & DISPLAY CAR PARK IN LANGTHWAITE.

PUBLIC HOUSE: RED LION Tel: 01748 884 218, CB INN Tel: 01748 884 567, BOTH IN LANGTHWAITE

TOTAL ASCENT: 358M

GRID REFERENCE: 005 024

CAFÉ: BRING SANDWICHES

Over Great Pinseat from Langthwaite

Directions – Over Great Pinseat
from Langthwaite

➊ From the car park in Langthwaite follow the road northwest towards Tan Hill for 3.5km, going past the church, the CB Inn and a right turn to Barnard Castle. **Ignore** the first bridleway to the left.

➋ Go past Moor Intake Farm up to the left and several houses and barns to the right. Take the next track to the **L** (GR 981 041) signposted *Bridleway only, no vehicles* (a cluster of houses in the village of Whaw lies down in the valley to the right).

➌ After 600m at a fork of tracks just before a round-roofed corrugated iron shed bear **L** to continue uphill and almost immediately bear **R** (in other words, do not go alongside the shed). Zig zag on the track passing above the spoil heap and climb steeply.

➍ The summit is marked by grassed over spoil heaps and small cairns of stones. Turn sharp **L** at a T-junction of tracks (GR 975 030) towards a larger spoil heap, not grassed over. The track soon improves dramatically for a very fine descent.

➎ At the T-junction with the road turn **R** then, **easy to miss:** shortly after a *1 in 5 gradient* sign and before a steep right-hand bend (GR 993 009) turn **L** uphill through a gate onto a broad grass and stone track signposted *Bridleway only, no vehicles*. Shortly, at a fork, bear **L** onto the wider, better defined path.

➏ Follow this for 2.2km to the T-junction with the road and turn **L** to return to Langthwaite.

◀🔗 **Making a day of it**
There is another ride starting from *Langthwaite* heading east over *Hurst Moor – see page 25*. At Fore Gill Gate, towards the end of the ride described here (at GR 992 009) you can easily link to the ride that explores *Reeth High Moor – see page 73*.

TYPICAL YORKSHIRE DRYSTONE WALLS LINE THE ROUTE

Two Short Rides from **Hardraw**   10km & 12km

Introduction

Two short rides – do them together, separately, link them to the Hawes route: the choice is yours. The Sedbusk ride climbs tarmac and is rewarded by a grassy track contouring to a descent straight down the hillside on grass then stone with the valley spread out like a tablecloth below. The Cotterdale loop climbs the ridge towards Great Shunner Fell on one of those tracks that challenge you not to dab between gates. A short plateau section leads to woodland and a fast descent on forest roads with an easily missed turn onto singletrack. Join tarmac and cruise back to the start.

The Rides

Sedbusk   10km

The Dales are full of steep lanes climbing up and over the fells linking one dale to the next: such is Buttertubs road north of Hardraw. A steep climb on tarmac takes you to the start of the off-road section – a mixture of stone and bumpy grass sections. The route takes a short section of wide, stone-based moorland motorway before careering off downhill through fields bounded by drystone walls.

Cotterdale   12km

Follow the Pennine Way northwest from Hardraw and you may encounter walkers who may expect you to ride, rather than push up the 260m climb. Perhaps I was lucky, but this is one of my favourite Dales climbs – always a challenge and never impossible. A brief grassy plateau with views into Cotterdale follows, before you plunge into woodland on forest roads dropping to the hamlet of Cotterdale.

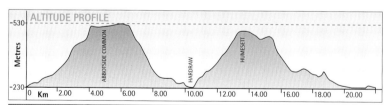

TWO SHORT RIDES FROM HARDRAW   **GRADE:** ▲

DISTANCE: 10KM (SEDBUSK) + 12KM (COTTERDALE)   **TOTAL ASCENT:** 310M (SEDBUSK) + 315M (COTTERDALE)

START/FINISH: HARDRAW, NORTH OF HAWES   **GRID REFERENCE:** 866 913

PARKING: PARKING ON THE VERGESIDE TO THE WEST OF HARDRAW VILLAGE

PUBLIC HOUSE: GREEN DRAGON,   **CAFE:** CART HORSE TEAROOM,

    HARDRAW Tel: 01969 667 392   HARDRAW Tel: 01969 667 691

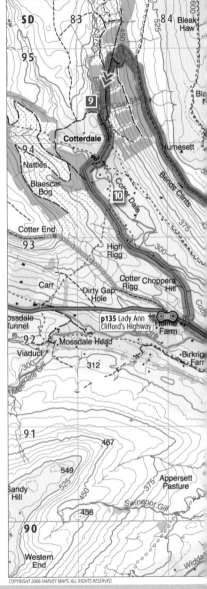

Two short rides from Hardraw

Directions – Two Short Rides from Hardraw

Ride 1: Abbotside Common and Sedbusk

⊙► Go east towards Askrigg through Hardraw village past the Cart Horse tearoom and Green Dragon pub. After 800m take the first road to the **L** signposted *Muker via Buttertubs*.

2 Climb steeply for 2.5km, cross a cattle grid and ignore a wide stone track to the right (with a metal barrier). After a further 800m and about 50m after passing a low crenellated wall to the left turn **R** by a *Bridleway to Sedbusk* signpost (GR 866 937). Soon join a better grass and stone track climbing towards the signpost on the horizon.

3 At the signpost leave the main stone track and bear **R** on the grassy track following the direction of the signpost. Very bumpy grass track for the next 800m waymarked by stone cairns and plain wooden posts. Join a better stone track and bear **L**.

4 After 1.5km on the moorland motorway turn **R** by a *Bridleway* signpost onto a grassy track. Go through a gate and descend on the obvious grassy track. At the T-junction with a wide stone track beyond the second gate turn **R** downhill.

5 Join tarmac in Sedbusk then at the T-junction with a letter box in the wall ahead turn **R**. At the T-junction with the outward route (Buttertubs road) turn **L** downhill. At the T-junction turn **R** signposted *Hardraw* to return to the starting point.

PHOTO: NICK COTTON

Ride 2: Hearne Top and Cotterdale

6 With your back to the Green Dragon pub in Hardraw turn **R**, cross the bridge over Hardraw Beck then turn **R** opposite *Focus on Felt* shop onto a wide gravel track signposted *Bridleway to Cotterdale & Fossdale Moss*.

7 After 1.5km, at a fork of tracks just after a gate by a *Pennine Way* signpost bear **L** on the steep, stonier track. Good challenge to ride the next 1.5km without a dab!

8 At a 3-way signpost continue **SA** on the *Bridleway to Cotterdale* (the Pennine Way goes off to the right). Soon reach the summit (Hearne Top) and a smooth grassy balcony path. The track along the northern edge of the forest is muddy in winter. Zig zag down through the forest following *Bridleway* signs.

9 **Very easy to miss:** after 1km, on the fast descent, keep an eye out for a *Bridleway* sign on the **right-hand side** of the track pointing you down off the main forest track onto singletrack (about 100m after the end of pheasant feeding bins). You may well miss this and arrive at the bridge over the river (East Gill) where there is a locked gate.

10 Cross the river via the footbridge, go through the cluster of houses in Cotterdale, cross a second bridge (over West Gill), climb, descend then climb again. At the T-junction with the A684 turn **L**. After almost 2km take the first road to the **L** signposted *Hardraw* to return to the start.

←👓 Making a day of it

The start of the ride up *Lady Ann Clifford's Highway* is at the junction of *Cotterdale* with the A684 – *see page 135*. There is a ride south from *Hawes*, also using the Pennine Way for its first section – *see page 103*.

HEADING EAST FROM LANGTHWAITE

East from **Langthwaite** onto **Hurst Moor**

15km

Introduction

This must be the only ride in Britain where you could see the instruction "Booze just off the route" and it has nothing to do with pubs. Yes, folks, there is a hamlet just east of Langthwaite called Booze. The stiff climb up from Langthwaite and the slightly tricky route finding up onto Peat Moor Green (avoiding Booze) is rewarded by a fine cruise over the heather-clad moorland, this off-road section ending with a fast 150m descent down to Schoolmaster Pasture.

But the best is yet to come – the climb west through Washfold and Hurst sets you up for one of the Dales' Top Ten Downhills, dropping down through the lead mine spoils to Storthwaite Hall. Yabba dabba dooo!™

The Ride

Leave the closely huddled houses of Langthwaite and take the steep tarmac lane climbing up above Arkengarthdale onto Scotty Hill. Leaving tarmac, a rough and ready section with a tumbledown wall and a vaguely defined path leads to a broad stone track that heads east across the remote expanse of Hurst Moor. Keep an eye out for the standing stone known as the Stony Man or St Andrew's Cross and, more importantly, for another stone with 'Hurst' painted on it. Fly down the fast descent to Schoolmaster Pasture, join tarmac and climb up past the tall old chimney at Hurst and off-road again. Now the real fun begins! Once you have found the start of the descent, it's five star entertainment all the way, dropping 200m through mining spoils and fields of pasture to the valley floor.

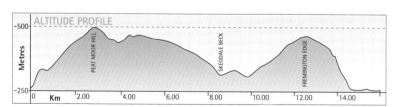

ALTITUDE PROFILE

-500

Metres

-250

0   Km   2.00   4.00   6.00   8.00   10.00   12.00   14.00

PEAT MOOR HILL · SKEGDALE BECK · FREMINGTON EDGE

EAST FROM LANGTHWAITE ONTO HURST MOOR   GRADE: ▲

DISTANCE: 15KM

START/FINISH: LANGTHWAITE, NORTHWEST OF REETH

PARKING: PAY & DISPLAY CAR PARK IN LANGTHWAITE

TOTAL ASCENT: 526M

GRID REFERENCE: 005 024

CAFÉ: BRING SANDWICHES

PUBLIC HOUSE: RED LION Tel: 01748 884 218, CB INN Tel: 01748 884 567, BOTH IN LANGTHWAITE

PHOTO: NICK COTTON

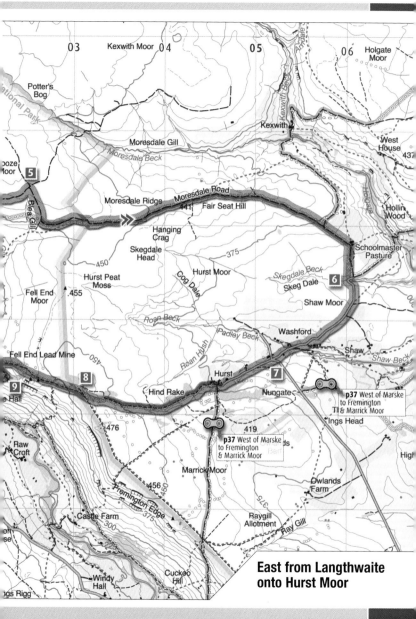

East from Langthwaite onto Hurst Moor

03 Kexwith Moor 04 05 06 Holgate Moor

Potter's Bog

National Park

Kexwith

Moresdale Gill

Moresdale Beck

West House 437

ooze Moor 5

Blea Gill

Moresdale Road

Moresdale Ridge 441 Fair Seat Hill

Hollin Wood

Hanging Crag

Schoolmaster Pasture

Skegdale Head

.450

375

Hurst Peat Moss

Hurst Moor

Cog Dale

Skegdale Beck

Skeg Dale 6

Fell End Moor .455

Shaw Moor

Roan Beck

Padley Beck

Washford

Fell End Lead Mine .450

Roan Hush

Shaw

Shaw Beck

9 8

Hind Rake

Hurst

Nungate 7

p37 West of Marske to Fremington T & Marrick Moor

e Hall

Ings Head

Raw Croft

.476

419

High

p37 West of Marske to Fremington & Marrick Moor

Marrick Moor

Owlands Farm

.456 450

Fremington Edge 375

Raygill Allotment

Ray Gill

375

Castle Farm 300

on se

Windy Hall

Cuckoo Hill

East from Langthwaite onto Hurst Moor

gs Rigg

Directions – East from Langthwaite onto Hurst Moor

➊ With your back to the Red Lion pub in Langthwaite turn **L** on the lane through the village, soon climbing steeply. Shortly after the summit the tarmac ends. After 300m, at the fork bear **L** on the upper track signposted *Fountain Farm*.

2 **Easy to miss:** at the gate 100m before the farm turn **L** steeply uphill on a grassy track by a ruin (GR 013 025). At the end of the rough, collapsed wall section bear **R** to go through a metal field gate and continue uphill.

3 After 300m, at the *Bridleway* sign, leave the main tractor track and bear **R** following the direction of the signpost alongside the wall to a gate near a small, low stone barn. Go steeply uphill on a faint track, soon turning **L** on a broad loose stone track then bearing **R** at fork of tracks by a wall corner to continue uphill towards a wooden post.

4 At a T-junction with a better track on a hairpin bend bear **R** (in effect go **SA**) then shortly **R** again.

5 Go past a low wooden building with a corrugated roof, continue climbing then at a fork of tracks after 800m bear **R** by a stone with *Hurst* written on it in white paint.

6 Great, easy descent over 4km, swooping down to a farmhouse (Schoolmaster Pasture). Continue descending, bear **R** at a T-junction to cross the bridge over Skegdale Beck and join tarmac, climbing the hill opposite.

7 Climb, descend to cross Padley Beck, climb again. At the T-junction by a telephone box turn **R**. Continue to the end of tarmac, passing a tall chimney to your left and go **SA** through a gate onto a track.

8 Go past the grouse butts, climb to the summit then bear **L** towards the gate in the wall near the junction of walls, fence and path (GR 031 023).

9 Great descent down through mining spoils. Go through a gate and continue downhill signposted *Langthwaite*. At the T-junction at the bottom by the buildings of Storthwaite Hall turn **R**. Cross the ford, attack the short climb then follow the main track parallel with the river (Arkle Beck) back to the start.

◄⚙⚙ Making a day of it

Another ride starts from *Langthwaite* itself, heading northwest on similar mining tracks over *Whaw Moor* – *see page 13*. The ride described here can link from its middle tarmac section at Washfold to the ride west of *Marske* that takes in *Marrick and High Fremington* – *see page 37*.

PETE DODD AND CLAIR LLOYD CLIMBING OUT OF GUNNERSIDE

Gunnerside & Melbecks Moor

12km

Introduction

Just when you thought you were getting into the remote wilds of Gunnerside Beck you discover the Machu Picchu of the Dales, a fine collection of old mining ruins from the days when lead was extracted extensively. As if this weren't enough, you climb the hill and could persuade yourself you had been dropped into some stony moonscape. It will all seem like a dream as you turn south back to Swaledale and the comforting sight of heather moors and grouse butts, then fields grazed by sheep and bounded by stone walls. And that's without telling you too much about the magic gate at the start...

The Ride

The route starts with one of the steepest road climbs in the Dales taking you high above Swaledale, soon contouring on a good stone track along the eastern slopes of Gunnerside Gill. Stone turns to a grassy track through ferns with the occasional tricky section and one washed-out part opposite Botcher Gill Nook. You soon come upon the old mining ruins making you realise how busy the valley must have been with the tramp of feet and horses in years gone by when the industry was in its heyday. The spoils can make route-finding tricky as you climb up out of Gunnerside Gill and onto the plateau of Melbecks Moor. With all the hard work now done it is a high level cruise followed by a fast stone and grass descent down into Swaledale.

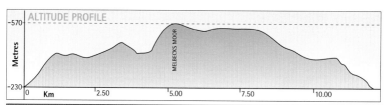

ALTITUDE PROFILE

MELBECKS MOOR

Metres

-570

-230

| 0 | Km | 2.50 | 5.00 | 7.50 | 10.00 |

GUNNERSIDE & MELBECKS MOOR

GRADE:

DISTANCE: 12KM

TOTAL ASCENT: 526M

START/FINISH: GUNNERSIDE, WEST OF REETH IN SWALEDALE

GRID REFERENCE: 951 983

PARKING: IN THE CENTRE OF THE VILLAGE OR ALONG THE B6270 ON THE EAST SIDE OF THE VILLAGE TOWARDS REETH.

CAFÉ: GHYLLFOOT CAFE, GUNNERSIDE Tel: 01748 886 239
OPEN MARCH TO OCTOBER, CLOSED TUESDAYS

PUBLIC HOUSE: KINGS HEAD, GUNNERSIDE
Tel: 01748 886 261

PUBLIC BRIDLEWAY

p143 North from
Muker to Tan Hill

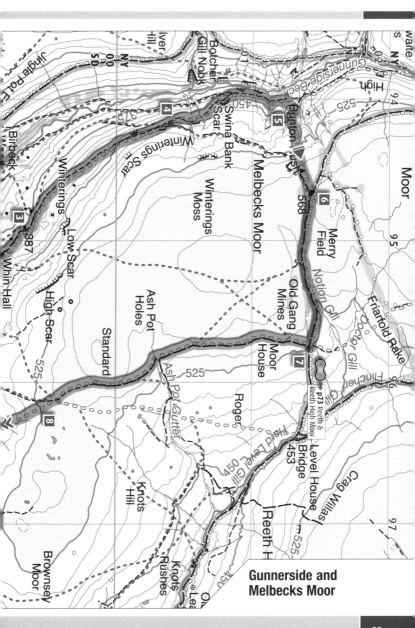

Gunnerside and
Melbecks Moor

Directions – Gunnerside and Melbecks Moor

S→ Follow the B6270 from the centre of Gunnerside as it climbs towards Reeth and Richmond. Near the end of the village bear L uphill onto a no through road through a grey metal gate operated by a push button.

2 Follow this very steep lane (160m climb) for 1.4km to the end of tarmac. Go through a gate and turn **L**, shortly taking the lower, **LH**, major track at a fork of tracks.

3 Follow the main track past two houses then, **easy to miss**, at a gap in the wall just past the second house, turn **R** onto a grassy track alongside the wall, soon climbing.

4 At a fork of tracks after 1.2km by a round, stone lime kiln with a rock face (Wintering Scar) up to your right (GR 942 003) bear **L** downhill. Some tricky singletrack and one short washed-out section opposite the narrow gully (Botcher Gill) on the other side of the valley.

5 At the end of the ruins bear **R** uphill on a stony track then shortly at a 4-way signpost (GR 940 013) turn sharp **R** uphill signposted *Surrender Bridge* on a smooth grassy track. After a short stone section arrive at an area of spoils where the path seems to peter out. Bear **L** following the grass strip straight up the hillside, climbing towards a tumbledown wall. At a T-junction with a better track turn **L**.

6 This climbs to a moonscape summit. Turn **R** by a cairn shortly after a square wooden fenced off area with a *Keep Out* sign on it.

7 **Easy to miss:** after heading east for 1.2km on this main broad track, towards the end of the moonscape, just beyond a spoil heap on the right, opposite a cairn on the left, with a long descent in view ahead, take the first major track uphill to the **R** OR towards a stone wall and ruins (GR 957 014).

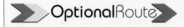

Optional Route

Or for a link to the *Reeth High Moor* ride (see page 73):
Continue **SA** downhill to the road then turn **R** and **L** signposted *Reeth*.

8 Superb stone-based roof-of-the-world track. Climb, descend briefly to cross a stream (Ash Pot Gutter) via a cobbled ford, climb again. Go past grouse butts to the right and left. The descent steepens and on a sharp right-hand bend just before the trail starts to climb again, bear **L** downhill on a broad, grassy track.

9 Go through a gate in a wall to continue downhill. At the T-junction with a better grass track turn **L** then just before a wall running straight down the hillside (with a gate in it) turn sharp **R** back on yourself down the grassy slope on a track towards cottages.

10 Emerge at tarmac to rejoin the outward route. Bear **L** downhill, go through the push button gate and turn **R** on the B6270 to return to the centre of Gunnerside.

◀ꝏ Making a day of it

There is an easy link from this ride to the *Reeth High Moor* ride from the moonscape plateau section down past Old Gang Smelting Mills – *see page 73*. To the west of *Gunnerside*, about 1.5km on tarmac links you to the *Muker* ride near Shore Gill (above Ivelet) – *see page 143*.

PHOTO: NICK COTTON

HIGH ABOVE HIGH FREMINGTON

West of **Marske** to **Fremington** & **Marrick Moor**

20km

Introduction

Marske is a small village just inside the National Park at its eastern end and is a fine starting point for exploring the bridleways to the north and west. The ride has two sections alongside the lovely River Swale, a steep climb up onto Fremington Edge offering fine views down to Reeth and Arkengarthdale and a short section of plateau cruising over heather-clad Marrick Moor. After a climb up from Helwith Bridge the final grass then stone track descent is a belter, dropping down into the valley formed by Marske Beck.

The Ride

A short road warm up from Marske leads to an attractive section alongside the River Swale before a climb up through sheep pastures. The pull of the River Swale brings you back down through Marrick and past the ruins of its old priory on a valley floor road to Fremington. A 250m climb up onto Fremington Edge earns brownie points. Marske is several km to the east and almost 300m lower so enjoy the three downhills, first across Marrick Moor to Hurst (stone) then Prys House to Helwith Bridge (mainly grass) and after one last climb, the final and best descent down into Marske.

Warning: *There is a tempting looking bridleway on the north side of Arkle Beck . At either end of the track it looks (and is) a wonderful easy ride, but the middle section is very narrow and overgrown, mainly on an unrideable camber and at times all but non-existent.*

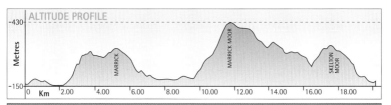

ALTITUDE PROFILE

(Metres, from -150 to -430; Km axis from 0 to 18.00, labels: MARRICK, MARRICK MOOR, SKELTON MOOR)

WEST OF MARSKE TO FREMINGTON & MARRICK MOOR GRADE: ▲

DISTANCE: 18KM

START/FINISH: MARSKE, EAST OF REETH

PARKING: PARKING NEAR THE BRIDGE OVER MARSKE BECK

CAFÉ: BRING SANDWICHES OR DETOUR TO REETH WHERE THERE IS LOTS OF CHOICE

TOTAL ASCENT: 699M

GRID REFERENCE: 104 004

PUBLIC HOUSE: LOTS OF CHOICE JUST OFF THE ROUTE IN REETH

**West of Marske
to Fremington &
Marrick Moor**

Directions – West of Marske to Fremington & Marrick Moor

➊ From the car parking area in Marske (GR 104 004) follow the road south towards Leyburn and Richmond for almost 1.5km.

➋ **Easy to miss:** go past a large farm on the left (Bushy Park). On the descent, about 50m after an *Other Danger* road sign (!) and a *Road liable to subsidence* road sign turn sharp **R** through a gate onto a broad stone track (opposite the first *Road bumps* sign). The track turns to tarmac.

➌ **Very easy to miss:** about 450m after the start of tarmac, on a climbing section, turn **R** onto a faint stone and grass track by a rounded wall end (there is a yellow dot on the wall). If you go past the farm at Low Oxque you have gone too far. Pass close to the barn (keep it to your right) on an overgrown track, go through a gate, soon bearing **L** towards a second gate leading into a steeply rising field. After 100m jink **L** then **R** through a bridlegate to join a better track with the fence now to your right.

➍ After 650m at a 2-way *Bridleway* signpost turn **L** to continue uphill, keeping the fence to your right. After 1.5km bear **R** on the lower track (GR 091 986).

➎ After almost 1km pass to the **L** of the farm (Nun Cote Nook) then at the T-junction with the road turn **L** uphill.

➏ Descend into Marrick. Ignore a no through road to the left on a right-hand bend then take the next lane to the **L** downhill opposite a slightly hidden telephone box. Shortly go round a right-hand bend then take the no through road to the **L** by a hay barn.

➐ Follow the lane/track round to the **R** then immediately turn **L** down a walled grassy track signposted *No vehicular access* (GR 078 979). Soon join a broad stone and grass track. Go through a farm (Wood House) and join tarmac, going past Marrick Priory.

➑ At the T-junction at the end of Marrick Priory road bear **L** for 700m. About 50m **before** the T-junction with the B6270 in Fremington turn **R** steeply uphill onto a narrow lane between a garage and houses. At the T-junction at the top of the climb turn **L** then follow the road round to the **R** to continue steeply uphill between a barn and a house in High Fremington.

9 Follow the steep tarmac lane to its end and onto a stone track. The gradient eases as you go through a gate in the boundary wall (GR 044 007). Superb track over Marrick Moor.

10 At the T-junction with the road by a tall chimney turn **R**. After 700m follow the road round a right-hand bend by a telephone box **ignoring** two closely spaced roads to the left. Climb steadily and take the first broad stone track to the **L** by a sign for *Prys House Farm, Bridleway*.

11 Go past the farm, through the farmyard and into a field with no obvious track. Follow the line of telegraph poles to a metal bridlegate in the wall ahead and continue through the next field alongside the wall to the left. Follow the zig zag track down to the river.

12 At the bottom of the descent but **before** the bridge, bear **R** steeply back up the hill on a loose stone track. Go over the summit and enjoy a great grassy then stone downhill with views down into the Marske Valley.

13 At the road turn **R**. At the T-junction just above Marske turn **L** downhill to return to the start.

← Making a day of it

There is another ride from *Marske*, a short loop using the final part of this ride in reverse – *see page 7*. At *Fremington* it would be easy to link to the *Reeth* rides – *see pages 73, 79 & 85* – and at *Hurst* to the ride east from *Langthwaite* – *see page 25*.

EASY RIDING OUTSIDE KIRKBY STEPHEN

Limestone Plateaux between
Kirkby Stephen & **Crosby Garrett**

20km

Introduction

Is Kirkby Stephen in the Yorkshire Dales National Park? No. Is this a good ride over nearby limestone tracks in beautiful scenery? Yes. Kirkby Stephen is quite a hub for the surrounding small villages so offers a fine array of pubs and cafés for your return to base. The ride links together quiet lanes, tracks through lush pasture, a climb over Smardale Fell opening up 360° views, the atmospheric crossing of Smardale Bridge and a wonderful breezy descent down to Crosby Garrett. A quick look at a map shows you that there are loads more bridleways stretching west from this ride towards Orton, Crosby Ravensworth and the M6, should you wish to explore this corridor between the two National Parks.

The Ride

Head west from the fleshpots of Kirkby Stephen south and west to the first off-road section running between walls, pastures and hedgerows down to the hamlet of Waitby. Climb up onto Smardale Fell for views of the Pennines to the north and east and the Howgills and Shap Fells to the south and west. This is one of those climbs that you should be able to ride, but a headwind, some soft ground or a little wheel spin may make a walk seem that bit easier. A grassy descent leads to views down Smardale Gill and then grass turns to stone through the farms either side of Brownber, once again climbing onto a grassy plateau on the west side of Scandal Beck. Whoosh down into Crosby Garrett on a fast stone track and quiet lanes back to the start.

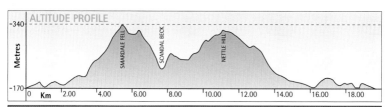

LIMESTONE PLATEAUX **GRADE:** ▲

DISTANCE: 20KM

TOTAL ASCENT: 438M

START/FINISH: WELL SIGNPOSTED FREE CAR PARK AT THE NORTH END OF KIRKBY STEPHEN ON THE ROAD TO SOULBY

GRID REFERENCE: 773 089

PARKING: AS ABOVE

PUBLIC HOUSE: LOTS OF CHOICE IN KIRKBY STEPHEN

CAFE: LOTS OF CHOICE IN KIRKBY STEPHEN

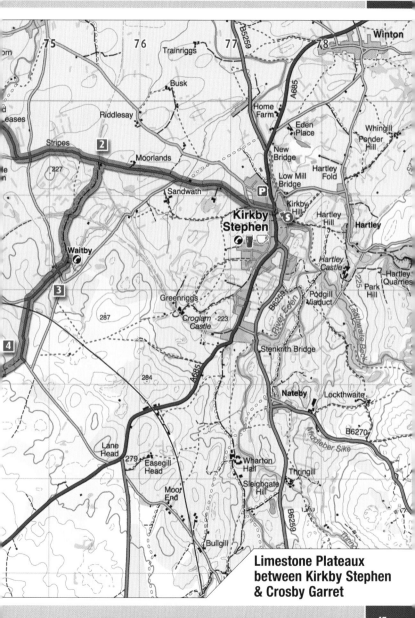

**Limestone Plateaux
between Kirkby Stephen
& Crosby Garret**

Directions – Limestone Plateaux between Kirkby Stephen and Crosby Garrett

➎ Exit Kirkby Stephen's free car park (on the road to Soulby), turn **L** then shortly after the school bear **L** onto the lane signposted *Waitby, Smardale*. After 800m at the bottom of a short descent bear **R** onto a lane signposted *Moorlands, Stripes*.

2 Go past Moorlands Farm to the right then immediately after the next house on the left (with white painted fence posts) turn **L** onto a broad stone track (no sign). Shortly after a sharp right-hand bend turn **L** between the stone walls of the old railway bridge supports. The next section may be muddy.

3 Keep bearing **R** to join tarmac near Waitby Farm. **Ignore** the first lane to the right signposted *Unsuitable for wide vehicles* then almost immediately at the T-junction turn **R** signposted *Smardale*. Climb and after 500m take the first lane to the **L**.

4 Gentle climb for 650m. On a sharp left-hand bend bear **R** through a gate into a field signposted *Coast to Coast, Bridleway to Brownber*. Follow the well-defined grass track climbing parallel with the wall on the right, bearing **R** as the wall swings round to the right.

5 Superb views in all directions from the highpoint. At a 4-way signpost at the bottom of a small dip continue **SA** signposted *Smardale Bridge, Coast to Coast*. Follow the wide grassy track parallel to the wall on the right. There are several parallel paths which all join up. The main track starts to descend steeply. Go through a gate onto a stone track. Descend to cross Smardale Bridge.

6 Steady climb after the bridge. Descend to rejoin tarmac by Friar's Bottom Farm, go through a gate then almost immediately turn **R** onto a narrow track between stone walls signposted *Bridleway to Ravenstonedale Moor*. The track broadens. Go through gates past the next farm and turn **R** onto a broad stone track between walls signposted *Bridleway to Bents*.

7 Follow this fine stone track right up to and through Bents Farm. Go past the house with its red painted windowsills then immediately **before** the final barn on the left turn **L** through two gates into a field towards a house set apart from the other buildings and towards a rocky outcrop.

8 Shortly, at the junction of tracks by a *Camping Barn* signpost continue **SA** uphill directly away from the farm (in other words, **do not** follow the track alongside the wall to the right). After 200m at a X-roads of grassy tracks turn **R** towards the telegraph poles on the horizon. Lots of parallel tracks all join, climbing to the highpoint.

9 The track becomes a fine stone-based descent. Join tarmac and go under the railway viaduct in Crosby Garrett. At the road signpost in the centre of the village bear **R** uphill towards the church signposted *Soulby, Kirkby Stephen*.

10 Climb up past the church then after 1km on a sharp left-hand bend bear **R** (no sign) onto the first lane you come across. At the T-junction turn **L** signposted *Soulby, Kirkby Stephen*. Rejoin the outward route then at the next T-junction turn **L** signposted *Kirkby Stephen*. At the final T-junction turn **R** signposted *Kirkby Stephen* to return to the free car park.

◄⚙◎ Making a day of it

As mentioned there are plenty more bridleways west of this ride towards the M6. Within the book the nearest ride lies south down the B6259 towards Garsdale where it is possible to access *Lady Ann Clifford's Highway* from the north end just beyond Outhgill – *see page 135.*

SECTION 2

Epics

Getting longer now – these loops will take a bit more time and effort. Not rides to be scared of, but definitely rides to be respected. Rather large hills and plenty of technical ground to cover mean that firstly, you're going to be out for a good few hours and secondly, you're going to have a really good time.

Epics

sponsored by

DALES
Mountain
BIKING

www.dalesmountainbiking.co.uk

HEATHER FIELDS ON GRINTON MOOR

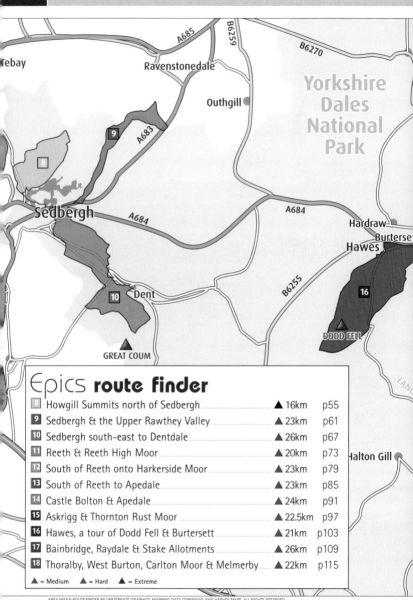

Epics **route finder**

▲ = Medium   ▲ = Hard   ▲ = Extreme

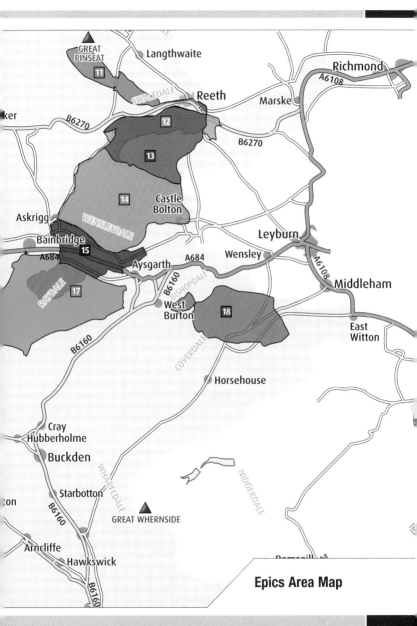

Epics Area Map

Howgill Summits north of Sedbergh 16km

Introduction

Ever thought how good the hills to the east of Shap Summit on the M6 look? Thought that they would be good to ride? Well come and find out: the tough climb up to the top of the Howgills from the attractive town of Sedbergh takes you into a mountain biking heaven of smooth tracks and a mind-blowing descent offering a fantastic taste of this lesser known range of hills, located between the Shap Fells of the Lake District to the west and the Yorkshire Dales to the east.

The Ride

A gentle start on Howgill Lane as it skirts the foot of the fells gives you a chance to contemplate the descent that will finish the ride. Moving off-road at Birkhaw Farm, the Howgills' enormous bulk looms large as you realise the scale of the task ahead – a 420m grassy climb (or push) up from Swarth Greaves Beck to Bram Rigg – the steepest and most sustained in this book. As you approach the top, sweating and cursing the author, things get worse: the track gets fainter and fainter until, as though someone has waved a wand, one of the most amazing tracks in the UK appears – a stone-based rollercoaster over a high plateau with stunning views. And if this isn't enough, the descent from Winder is a whoop-with-joy number as you swoop down smooth grassy tracks back to Howgill Lane and Sedbergh.

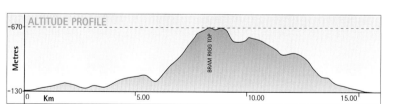

ALTITUDE PROFILE

BRAM RIGG TOP

Metres

670

130

0   Km   5.00   10.00   15.00

HOWGILL SUMMITS NORTH OF SEDBERGH	GRADE: ▲
DISTANCE: 16KM	**TOTAL ASCENT:** 765M
START/FINISH: SEDBERGH POST OFFICE	**GRID REFERENCE:** 657 918
PARKING: FREE PARKING IN SEDBERGH ON THE ROAD TOWARDS DENT	
CAFÉ: LOTS OF CHOICE IN SEDBERGH	**PUBLIC HOUSE:** LOTS OF CHOICE IN SEDBERGH

BW BRANT FELL 3

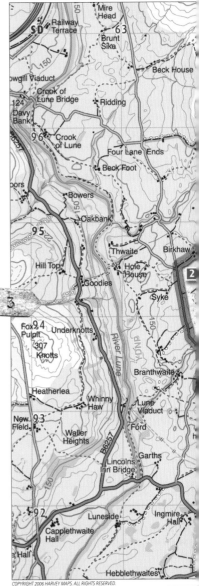

**Howgill Summits
north of Sedbergh**

Directions – Howgill Summits
north of Sedbergh

5 With your back to the Post Office in the centre of Sedbergh turn **R** then first **R** uphill. Follow this lane along the foot of the hills to the right. After 2km **ignore** the bridleway to the right signposted *Brant Fells* (this is the return route).

2 **Easy to miss:** after a further 2km, opposite a tarmac lane to the left signposted *Thwaite*, turn **R** on a wide, smooth gravel track (GR 636 945) signposted *Birkhaw*. Pass between farm buildings and through a gate signposted *Bridleway only* onto a gently rising track through woodland.

3 Follow the track alongside a stone wall. With a conifer plantation 100m to your right, turn **L** on a fairly level grass and stone track with the wall to your left. Continue in the same direction through double gates then at a choice of tracks stay on the **left-hand** track with the gentlest gradient closest to the wall.

4 Descend to cross two streams (Swarth Greaves Beck and Bram Rigg Beck) via a ford following the obvious track as it swings up and to the **R**. Shortly after the second stream crossing the bridleway follows a wide grassy track leading steeply **R** off the stone track. Very steep 2.5km grassy climb (420m of ascent) with one zig zag section.

5 As the gradient eases the path becomes indistinct. Do not fear! Continue in the same direction over the brow and join an amazing stone track. Turn **R** onto this superb track with amazing views which you follow for 4km generally descending (with the odd short climb) over Bram Rigg, Calders, Rowantree Grains and Arant Haw to the trig point on Winder.

6 Bear **R** at the trig point on at first a faint grassy track which soon becomes more defined. What a descent! At the T-junction with the wall turn **R** for 100m then turn **L** downhill through a gate onto a rough stone track that soon improves. At the road turn **L** to return to Sedbergh.

◂🚲 Making a day of it

There are two other rides starting from *Sedbergh*: one goes southeast towards *Dentdale – see page 61* – and the other northeast up the *Rawthey Valley – see page 61*.

NB The tempting-looking bridleway shown on the map dropping north down Bowderdale from the top of The Calf is a bit of a disappointment – often narrow, sunken, boggy or filled with loose rubble.

PETE DODD AND ROSEMARY LAKIN EXPERIENCING DALES SINGLETRACK

Sedbergh and the Upper Rawthey Valley

23km

Introduction

There is more than a hint of the Welsh Borders on this relatively easy ride that skirts rather than climbs the smooth grassy bulk of the Howgills which lie to the west. The fine views up into the vast bowl formed by Cautley Spout are repeated in the second half of the ride once you have climbed up onto the east side of the valley. There is a great café/ tea stop at Cross Keys, a 'dry' pub about halfway along the ride.

The Ride

Leave Sedbergh northeast on the A683, one of Cumbria's quietest A-roads, before diving off onto a narrow lane bordered by high hedgerows. Tarmac turns to track at Thursgill Farm followed by a variety of surfaces, starting and finishing with fine stone tracks but with some overgrown, narrow sections and tricky stream crossings. The end of this section gives stunning views up towards the dramatic waterfall of Cautley Spout. Cross the bridge over the River Rawthey, fill up with cakes and coffee at the Cross Keys café, rejoin tarmac and peel off again into the wilds towards Uldale House. Drop through woodland to cross the infant River Rawthey, climb to a stone and grass track (soft in winter) and contour around the valley to zip down to the main road and back to Sedbergh.

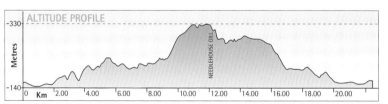

ALTITUDE PROFILE

NEEDLEHOUSE GILL

SEDBERGH AND THE UPPER RAWTHEY VALLEY	**GRADE:** ▲
DISTANCE: 23KM	**TOTAL ASCENT:** 533M
START/FINISH: SEDBERGH POST OFFICE	**GRID REFERENCE:** 657 918
PARKING: FREE PARKING IN SEDBERGH ON THE ROAD TOWARDS DENT	
CAFÉ: EXCELLENT REFRESHMENTS AT THE CROSS KEYS ON THE A683 Tel: 01539 620 284	
PUBLIC HOUSE: LOTS OF CHOICE IN SEDBERGH	

PHOTO: NICK COTTON

**Sedbergh and the
Upper Rawthey Valley**

Directions – Sedbergh and the Upper Rawthey Valley

➲ From the Post Office in the centre of Sedbergh follow Finkle Street towards Dent past the Red Lion pub then at the mini-roundabout turn **L** onto Back Lane signposted *Hawes, Kirkby Stephen*.

2 Easy to miss: about 800m after the end of the speed limit after leaving Sedbergh on the A683, take the second of two closely spaced lanes to the **L** (no sign on either – GR 672 924). After 1.4km, at the end of the tarmac, go **SA** through a gate by the farm (Thursgill) to continue in the same direction on a stone and grass track.

3 The next 4km are a mix of excellent riding and occasionally overgrown, narrow or rough sections. Start with a great track through woodland. Cross a bridge over Hobdale Beck and climb steeply on a concrete and grass track to Fawcett Bank. Follow white arrows through a gate onto a wide grass track.

4 About 3km after Fawcett Bank on a variety of riding surfaces, descend to cross the footbridge over the stream coming from Cautley Spout, go **SA** for 50m then turn **R** on a more defined track, which becomes a smooth gravel track. Cross the River Rawthey via a narrow footbridge, climb to the A683 and turn **L** (OR, for the highly recommended Cross Keys café and tearoom, turn **R** for 200m).

5 After 2.7km on the A683, immediately after crossing a wide stone bridge over the River Rawthey, turn **R** signposted *Uldale Fell End*. Follow the road for 1.2km then shortly after passing houses to the right and left, turn **R** onto a no through road signposted *Uldale*.

6 After 1.5km, at a fork take the upper **LH** tarmac lane signposted *Bridleway, Uldale House* (the right-hand fork leads to Needle House). Descend to cross Needlehouse Gill, climb, then at the brow of the hill and at the edge of the woodland turn **R** through a gate signposted *Bridleway to Bluecaster*. Go down through woodland to cross Rawthey Gill via a wooden bridge and turn **R** uphill onto a narrow stone track.

7 The next 2km has lots of boggy bits which will be very wet from late autumn to late spring. Join a better track which also has some rough sections with stream crossings. The track was originally built along a sunken course which has filled up with reeds so the best line is often to the side of this.

8 Join tarmac after passing a wonderfully located house (Bluecaster Side) on the right. Descend to the road and turn **L**. Follow the A683 for 6km back into Sedbergh.

⬅️🔗 Making a day of it

Two other rides start from *Sedbergh* – a spectacular challenge climbing to the top of the Howgills – *see page 55* – and a low level one over to *Dentdale* – *see page 67*.

NB the bridleways heading north from Cross Keys towards Adamthwaite on the west side of the A683 are very hard work, badly drained and poorly maintained.

WE'RE NOT POSING... HONEST!

Sedbergh south-east to **Dentdale**   26km

Introduction

Dent has two pubs, three cafés and a brewery – not a bad destination for a trip! The ride is an exploration of the western end of Dentdale, one of the softer, more wooded valleys of the Yorkshire Dales. There's a ford of unknown depth, some easy and some tough lane riding, a long section on a contouring green lane much loved by our scramble bike pals, and a bone-shaking descent down Nun House Outrake. The section up above Lunds feels a lot more remote than its proximity to civilisation would suggest, with panoramic views north towards the Howgills.

The Ride

Head south from Sedbergh, through Millthrop and join the Dales Way, a long-distance trail from Ilkley to Windermere. Drop past Gap Wood and take your pick – the ford through the River Dee (is it really that deep?), or the footbridge. The gentle gradients of the lane along the valley give way to a steep tarmac climb to the start of a long, walled section on a contouring track. (At the time of writing, restoration works are underway to repair motorbike damage.) Turn off the main trail to rattle your teeth out on the descent of Nun House Outrake on your way down to Deepdale. Recross the Dee and climb steeply to the end of the tarmac at Lunds, negotiating a series of gates and occasional reedy patches (soft in winter) before crossing the watershed and dropping back down to the Rawthey Valley and Sedbergh.

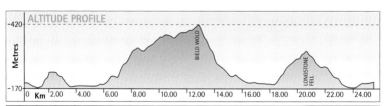

SEDBERGH SOUTH-EAST TO DENTDALE	GRADE: ▲
DISTANCE: 26KM	**TOTAL ASCENT:** 719M
START/FINISH: SEDBERGH POST OFFICE	**GRID REFERENCE:** 657 918
PARKING: FREE PARKING IN SEDBERGH ON THE ROAD TOWARDS DENT	
CAFÉ: LOTS OF CHOICE IN SEDBERGH AND DENT	**PUBLIC HOUSE:** LOTS OF CHOICE IN SEDBERGH AND DENT

Sedbergh south-east to Dentdale

Directions – Sedbergh south-east to Dentdale

> From the Post Office in the centre of Sedbergh follow Finkle Street towards Dent past the Red Lion pub and go **SA** at the mini-roundabout. After 800m cross the bridge over the River Rawthey and take the first lane to the **L** signposted *Millthrop*. Shortly, at the T-junction in Millthrop turn **R** then on a right-hand bend bear **L** onto a track signposted *Bridleway to Frostrow Fell*.

2 Short loose stone section. Climb, descend briefly to cross a small stream then at a fork bear **L** signposted *Dales Way* (there is a footpath to the right). Follow *Bridleway* and *Dales Way* signs along a mainly grassy track. Go through a lovely woodland section (Gap Wood) then past Gap Farm on a better stone track, descending and bearing **R**.

3 At the T-junction of stone tracks turn **R** to continue downhill. At the T-junction with the road turn **L** then **R** onto a track signposted *Bridleway to Brackensgill*. Cross the river via the ford (deep!) or the footbridge. At the road turn **L**.

4 After 3.5km take the first proper road to the **R** ⟩OR⟩ (in other words, not no through roads/farm drives) signposted *Barbon, Kirkby Lonsdale* to climb steeply. After 2km and shortly after the summit turn **L** onto a broad stone track signposted *Bridleway to Dent, Nun House and High Moss*.

5 Follow this mixed quality track (likely to be hard work in winter) for the next 4.25km. On a sharp right-hand bend as the gradient suddenly steepens turn **L** downhill signposted *Nun House Outrake*.

6 Some very rubbly sections on the downhill. A concrete drive starts by the farm. At the T-junction with the road turn **L**. At the T-junction with a more major road by a triangle of grass turn **L** signposted *Gawthrop, Sedbergh*.

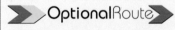
⟩⟩Optional Route⟩

Or for a Short Cut
>   Continue **SA** towards Dent, shortly at the T-junction turn **L** towards Sedbergh, cross the bridge over the River Dee then after 200m turn **R** onto a no through road (rejoin at **9**)

7 Soon after passing the Post Office in Dent, and immediately after the George & Dragon pub, turn **R** signposted *Hawes* to go past the church. Descend to cross the River Dee and after 200m turn sharp **L** onto a lane signposted *Road liable to flooding*.

8 After 1.75km at the T-junction with a busier road bear **R** (in effect **SA**) then, ignoring the first footpath/track on the right, after 100m take the next **R** onto a no through road (by a *Sedbergh 4 ½* signpost).

9 Climb to the end of the tarmac. About 100m after passing the gravel drive to Rawridding Farm to the left take the **left-hand** fork onto a grass and tarmac track. With Lunds Farm ahead turn **L** signposted *Footpath to Sedbergh*, follow past barns and go through four gates in quick succession.

10 At first the track is rough and overgrown but becomes a grass track between stone walls with one boggy section. Continue in the same direction through two more gates by a sheepfold then through a reedy patch climbing and going **SA** at a 3-way *Bridleway to Sedbergh* signpost following the wall to the left.

11 Go through a gate and turn **L** alongside the wall (a *Bridleway to Lunds* signpost points back where you have come from). Mixed quality track over next 2.5km turns to tarmac by Side Farm.

12 Follow the tarmac lane to the A684 and turn **L**. At the next T-junction (with the A683) turn **L** to return to the start.

◀️⊚⊙ Making a day of it

At the eastern end of the ride you are very close (1km) to the route that starts at *Ribblehead, Dentdale & Great Knoutberry Hill* route from **Yorkshire Dales Mountain Biking – The South Dales**, the companion guide to this book. Two other rides start from *Sedbergh*, one northeast up the *Rawthey Valley – see page 61*, the other a spectacular challenge climbing to the top of the *Howgills – see page 55*.

EVEN THE ROAD RIDING IS FUN!

Reeth & Reeth High Moor

Introduction

Set around a handsome green, Reeth is an excellent centre to be based for a few days for an exploration of the rides that fan out in all directions from the village. The next village to the west along Swaledale is Healaugh and continuing west from here across fields of heather you soon join the superb stone mining tracks describing a loop around Reeth High Moor. With the sun out and the wind behind you, the descent past Old Gang Smelting Mills is one of those easy-peasy glides where you almost feel you are floating. All over too soon!

The Ride

Warm up those legs along the B6270 between Reeth and Healaugh to prepare yourself for the steep tarmac climb north out of the village. The bridleway northwest to Foregill Gate across the heather moor is at times difficult to follow as there are several tracks on the ground and very few signs. Still, it is almost all rideable and after a swift down then up to cross Bleaberry Gill you are onto the start of the very fine stone track leading northwest and climbing to 570m past some very large and very remote sheepfolds. What goes up... must drop 360m back to Reeth, on a rough stone track criss-crossing Flincher Gill down to the very handsome Level House Bridge then on a smooth stone beauty past the ruins of Old Gang Smelting Mills down to road and a lovely quiet lane down into the lush green splendours of Swaledale.

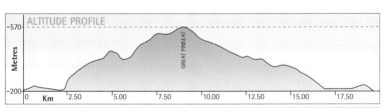

ALTITUDE PROFILE

Metres

570

200

0   Km   2.50   5.00   7.50   10.00   12.50   15.00   17.50

GREAT PINSEAT

REETH & REETH HIGH MOOR   GRADE: ▲

DISTANCE: 20KM

START/FINISH: REETH, SWALEDALE

PARKING: AROUND THE GREEN IN REETH

CAFÉ: NONE EN ROUTE, LOTS OF CHOICE IN REETH

TOTAL ASCENT: 586M

GRID REFERENCE: 038 993

PUBLIC HOUSE: LOTS OF CHOICE IN REETH

Reeth &
Reeth High Moor

Directions – Reeth & Reeth High Moor

1 Follow the B6270 west out of Reeth towards Healaugh and Keld.

2 After 2km, in Healaugh, turn **R** on the minor lane leading north out of the village by the village noticeboard and continue straight uphill through a gate on the no through road. The steep tarmac ends at a house (Thirns). At the fork of tracks bear **R** steeply uphill on the grass and stone track **leaving** the major, newer track.

3 Shortly after passing a walled field to the left the main track swings **R** uphill away from the wall (GR 010 996). **Easy to miss:** 200m after this bear **R** uphill away from the main track onto a grassy track running parallel with another walled enclosure up to the right. (This may be waymarked with a post with a blue arrow).

4 Follow this track northwest for 2km, go through the gate at Fore Gill Gate and turn **L** onto the road. Descend steeply to cross the ford then climb. Shortly after the brow turn **R** onto a broad stone track signposted *Bridleway*.

5 The track climbs steadily and gets rougher with some reedy patches. Go past large stone sheepfolds (GR 974 023) and towards the white/brown slag heaps ahead. Descend from the summit on Great Pinseat to cross then recross the stream (Flincher Gill).

6 At the T-junction with the main track by the very fine stone Level House Bridge turn **L**. Superb fast descent past Old Gang Smelting Mill ruins.

7 At the road turn **R** downhill to cross the stream (Old Gang Beck) then take the first road **L** signposted *Reeth*. After 3.5km, at the T-junction with the B6270 turn **L** through Healaugh and return to Reeth.

⟜ Making a day of it

Easily links from Level House Bridge (GR 964 014) west to the *Gunnerside* ride – *see page 31* – or at Fore Gill Gate (GR 992 009) to the *Langthwaite* ride – *see page 13*. There are two other rides heading south from *Reeth* itself – *see pages 79 & 85* – and the option to link with the *Marske* ride at *High Fremington* – *see page 37*.

SPRINGTIME IN SWALEDALE

South of **Reeth** onto **Harkerside Moor**

23km

Introduction

There is a mass of bridleways south of Reeth on the other side of the River Swale up onto Harkerside Moor. The route described here takes the only main east–west bridleway across the north-facing slopes, but the myriad tracks on the ground can make route finding tricky. The first third of the ride runs along the valley, close to the river, with an attractive cobbled section (likely to be under water after heavy rain) followed by a track covered by a canopy of broadleaf trees to Low Houses. The climb from here is long and steep, 320m up from the river to the high moorland, but the reward is an undulating 'balcony' track across Harkerside Moor and a fast descent via Cogden Hall back down to the valley floor.

The Ride

Cross the River Swale via Grinton Bridge and turn west along the river, on lane, stone track, grass track and even a newly-built cobbled section right alongside the water. After a short distance on tarmac plunge back off-road under a green canopy all the way to Low Houses, where the **big climb** starts. Climb exceedingly steeply on grass and rough stone up to the Askrigg road then on a better, broad stone track up to the highpoint of the ride. If all is well you will have the wind on your back and a predominantly downhill ride over the next 10km as you cross the heather slopes of Harkerside Moor to the Redmire road then drop steeply down the hillside past Cogden Hall with fabulous views to Reeth.

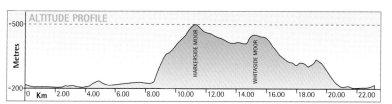

ALTITUDE PROFILE

| | HARKERSIDE MOOR | WHITASIDE MOOR |

Metres

-500
-200

0 Km 2.00 4.00 6.00 8.00 10.00 12.00 14.00 16.00 18.00 20.00 22.00

SOUTH OF REETH ONTO HARKERSIDE MOOR

GRADE: ▲

DISTANCE: 23KM

TOTAL ASCENT: 635M

START/FINISH: REETH

GRID REFERENCE: 038 993

PARKING: AROUND THE GREEN IN THE CENTRE OF REETH

CAFÉ: LOTS OF CHOICE IN REETH

PUBLIC HOUSE: LOTS OF CHOICE IN REETH

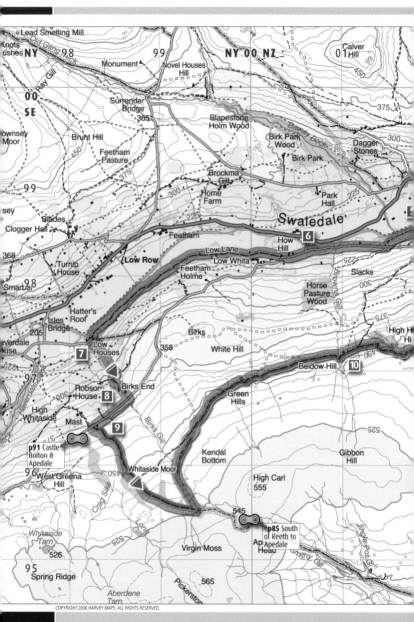

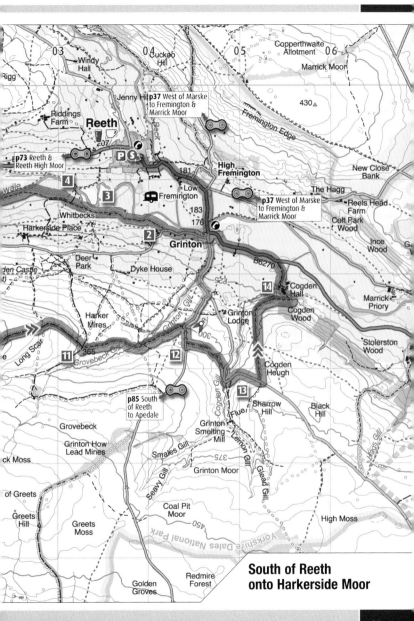

**South of Reeth
onto Harkerside Moor**

Directions – South of Reeth
onto Harkerside Moor

❻ From the centre of Reeth follow the B6270 southeast to Grinton for 1.5km.

2 Cross the bridge over the River Swale then on the sharp left-hand bend by the Bridge Inn bear **R** (in effect **SA**) towards *Redmire, Leyburn* then shortly turn first **R** signposted *Harkerside*. After 300m as the road swings sharp left uphill by a wooden bench bear **R** onto a narrow gravel track signposted *Bridleway*.

3 Go through several gates following the generally level path. Once out of the enclosed section, do **not** go towards the suspension footbridge but continue parallel with the river and about 200m away from it, soon joining a well-defined grass and stone track.

4 **Easy to miss:** at the end of the wall on the right, with a stone barn about 250m ahead, bear **R** through a bridlegate by a blue-topped post onto a grassy track diagonally across the field towards the river. There is a short cobbled section alongside the river.

5 After 1km leave the river immediately beyond a bridlegate with a yellow paint spot (GR 015 983) to bear **L** uphill on a grassy track. Follow this grassy track as it contours then climbs again to join the road. Turn **R** on the road.

6 **Ignore** a right (road) turn to Reeth, then shortly, on a sharp left-hand bend by the Low Row Bunk House, bear **R** onto a wide stone track signposted *Unsuitable for motors*.

7 Follow this wooded enclosed track for 2.5km. At Low Houses Farm continue **SA** for 30m past the stone house and barn on the left then turn **L** steeply uphill through a gate adjacent to a corrugated iron lean-to barn onto a very steep grassy track going straight up the hillside.

8 At a T-junction with a better track (GR 985 969) turn **R** then soon swing **L** on a grassy track between walls (in other words, do **not** follow the stone track across the bridge). Final steep section at the top.

9 At the T-junction with the road turn **R** for 500m. Immediately after a low stone 'garage' with wooden doors turn **L** uphill signposted *Bridleway to Castle Bolton*. Climb steeply for 1.8km and follow the main track as it turns sharp **L** and levels out by a wooden post (GR 993 955).

10. Excellent stone track – a 'balcony' path with undulations. After 3km at a fork of tracks shortly after passing a wooden hut to the left (just after crossing the gully formed by Browna Gill) bear **R** on the upper track (GR 012 972). A short steep zig zag leads to the highpoint on High Harker Hill by a lonesome *Bridleway* signpost. Continue heading east.

11. **Easy to miss:** after a steep descent, at a T-junction of stone tracks with a shooting lodge about 800m away to the right, continue **SA** on a well-defined grassy track. There is a large, half-buried, round, black plastic drainage pipe at this junction (GR 033 972).

12. Drop down to cross the streambed of Grovebeck Gill near some newly planted trees, go through a gate and climb. At the T-junction with the road turn **R*** uphill. **Easy to miss:** climb on tarmac for 200m, then shortly after passing a white (upside down) *Slow* sign painted on the road turn **L** onto a faint, broad, level, grassy track.

   * ⤷OR turn **L** for a short cut back to Reeth.

13. Generally downhill. At the T-junction with the road turn **R** to cross the bridge over Cogden Gill and climb steeply. After 600m turn **L** through a gate onto a track signposted *Bridleway, no vehicles*.

14. Fine track with good Reeth views. At the fork of tracks by the telegraph poles turn **L** sharply downhill round a hairpin bend. Descend through the farmyard of Cogden Hall. At the B6270 turn **L** to return to the start.

◄⊙⊙ Making a day of it

Two other rides start from *Reeth*, one south to *Apedale* – see page 85 – the other west to *Healaugh* and *High Reeth Moor* – see page 73. There is an easy link to the *Marske* ride at *Fremington*, just east of *Reeth* – see page 37. *Langthwaite*, with two more rides – see pages 13 & 25 – is only 4km up *Arkengarthdale* to the northwest.

RIDING ALONG THE RIVER SWALE

South of **Reeth** to **Apedale**

23km

Introduction

Apedale must feature in every mountain bike guide written about the Dales – a good broad stone track climbing 170m from the road access points at either end to a 550m highpoint with massively enjoyable descents following the climbs. No surprise then that it is also featured in another ride in the book, south to Castle Bolton. You have to work for your enjoyment, with a tough ascent from Grinton to Greets Hill but the rest is pretty straightforward. Dropping down off the moor down into Swaledale brings its own challenges and rewards finishing with one of the few tracks suitable for novices in the area, from Low Houses to Grinton.

The Ride

The climbing is all in the first half of the ride, split into three sections. First up is a 240m tarmac climb along the Castle Bolton road. Next, 90m up a rough stone track to the first summit on Greets Hill and finally, after a fast descent to the crossroads at Dent's Houses, a 170m climb to the high point of the ride at the watershed south of High Carl. Enjoy the descent and the views across to Crackpot on the other side of the valley. The most technical bits of the ride come after crossing the Askrigg road, although, as so often in the Dales, this is not a series of perfect drop offs but a steep and rubbly challenge where you hope that the front end of your bike knows what it's doing! Down at the valley bottom, follow the track east under a canopy of trees and briefly join tarmac before a final riverside amble back to Grinton and Reeth.

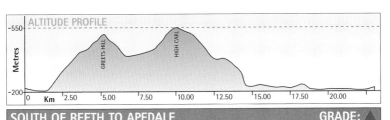

ALTITUDE PROFILE

550

Metres

GREETS HILL

HIGH CARL

-200

| 0 | Km | 2.50 | 5.00 | 7.50 | 10.00 | 12.50 | 15.00 | 17.50 | 20.00 |

SOUTH OF REETH TO APEDALE

GRADE: ▲

DISTANCE: 23KM

START/FINISH: REETH

PARKING: AROUND THE GREEN IN THE CENTRE OF REETH

CAFÉ: LOTS OF CHOICE IN REETH

TOTAL ASCENT: 653M

GRID REFERENCE: 038 993

PUBLIC HOUSE: LOTS OF CHOICE IN REETH

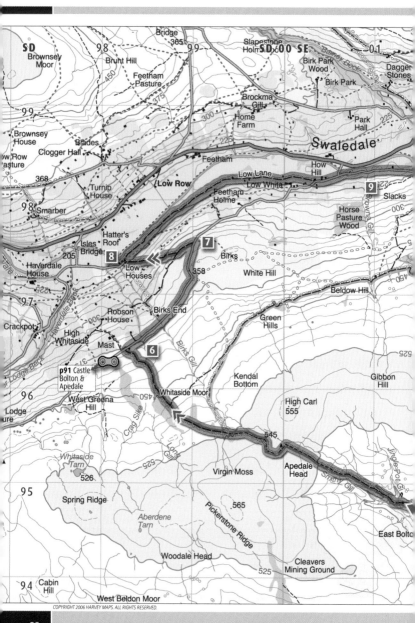

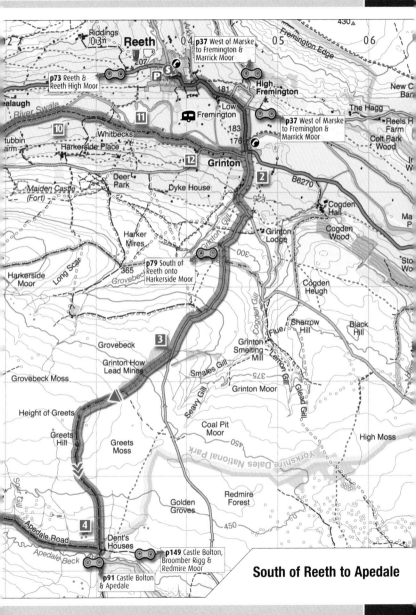

South of Reeth to Apedale

Directions – South of Reeth to Apedale

⑥ From the centre of Reeth follow the B6270 southeast to Grinton for 1.5km.

② Cross the bridge over the River Swale then on the sharp left-hand bend by the Bridge Inn bear **R** (in effect **SA**) towards *Redmire, Leyburn*. Climb for 1km then shortly after the cattlegrid take the first road to the **R**. Continue climbing steeply for almost 2km **ignoring** several bridleways to the right.

③ Shortly after the gradient eases and just before a gravel parking area on the right bear **R** on a faint grassy track signposted *Bridleway* (GR 038 963). The path is a bit vague but continue southwest uphill in the same direction to pass a cairn then head towards distinctive double cairns on the horizon.

④ Descend from the summit for 1.5km to a X-roads of tracks near a corrugated iron barn and turn **R** on a broad stone track.

⑤ After 1.3km at a fork of tracks bear **R** on the upper track (in other words, do **not** cross Apedale Beck). One very steep climb.

⑥ Descend from the summit for 2.5km to the road and turn **R**. After 500m **ignore** the bridleway to the left by the cattlegrid.

⑦ **Easy to miss:** after a further 1km the gradient steepens then shortly after the start of a left-hand bend by a wooden bench and a *Footpath* sign to the right turn sharp **L** through a gate onto a wide track (GR 990 975).

⑧ Shortly, bear **R** at a fork and continue bearing **R**. At the T-junction at the bottom by Low Houses farm buildings turn **R** signposted *Grinton*. Superb enclosed track under a canopy of trees.

⑨ At the road bear **L** and **ignore** a road to Reeth to the left. Cross the cattlegrid and climb. Soon after passing beneath power lines carried by telegraph poles turn **L** onto a grassy track signposted *Grinton* (NB **not** the footpath just before this). Good grassy descent to the river.

10 Pass over a cobbled section. **Easy to miss:** immediately after passing through a bridlegate adjacent to a stile in a wooden fence leave the riverside embankment path (GR 027 989) and drop down **R** onto a parallel path which soon bears away to the **R** diagonally to a gate in the far corner of the field.

11 At a better track turn **L**. As the track swings left towards a suspension bridge/footbridge continue **SA** on a faint grassy track. This soon becomes more defined.

12 At the road bear **L** then at the T-junction near the church in Grinton turn **L**. Shortly at the junction with the B6270 bear **L** (in effect **SA**) by the Bridge Inn to return to Reeth.

←⚙ Making a day of it

Two other rides start from *Reeth – see pages 73 & 85 –* and two more from nearby *Langthwaite – see pages 13 & 25.* The ride from *Marske* can be joined at *Fremington – see page 37.*

CASTLE BOLTON

Castle Bolton & Apedale

24km

Introduction

The first 10km of the ride from Castle Bolton to the road above Askrigg is one of the longest unbroken sections of off-road in the whole of the National Park. Running along the north side of Wensleydale, it climbs and dips past farms and broadleaf copses, old mining ruins and between drystone walls to reach the road above Askrigg. After a steep road climb, the second off-road treat runs along Apedale – quintessential Yorkshire Dales mountain biking on an excellent stone track. The final descent sees you rattle down to the big castle and a bit of culture...

The Ride

Head west from the dramatic Castle Bolton, climbing steadily with ever finer views of Wensleydale opening up to the south and west. The trail runs over a mixture of surfaces from broad stone to grass to reedy grass and continues switching between all three. A 200m climb on tarmac takes you over the second highest road pass in the Dales (the highest is between Hawes and Langstrothdale) and down towards Swaledale. Unfortunately, the next descent is on tarmac, but as it does encourage you to hit Mach 4 on the way down, it's not too bad! Pay for your speedy descent on the climb up over Whitaside Moor and set up for the heavenly descent down Apedale to the bleak crossroads at Dent's Houses. Turn right for the final short 40m climb setting you up for the swoop back down to the start.

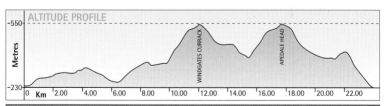

ALTITUDE PROFILE

Metres

-550
-230

0 Km 2.00 4.00 6.00 8.00 10.00 12.00 14.00 16.00 18.00 20.00 22.00

WINDGATES CURRACK

APEDALE HEAD

CASTLE BOLTON & APEDALE   GRADE: ▲

DISTANCE: 24KM
START/FINISH: CASTLE BOLTON
PARKING: BY BOLTON CASTLE
PUBLIC HOUSE: NEAREST PUBS ARE IN REDMIRE, CARPERBY AND ASKRIGG
TOTAL ASCENT: 662M
GRID REFERENCE: 033 919
CAFÉ: NEAREST OPTIONS ARE IN ASKRIGG

Castle Bolton & Apedale

Directions – Castle Bolton & Apedale

➊ Exit the car park opposite Bolton Castle and turn **R** through the gate signposted *Askrigg*. Follow this broad smooth stone track through a whole series of gates. The waymarking is with yellow dots, arrows and yellow-tipped posts.

2 After 1.4km pass between barns and go through a gate onto a slightly rougher track with a wall to the left. After 400m follow the main track through a gate in the wall to the left, soon running through woodland parallel to the wall. After the next gate the track turns to grass and the wall is once again to the left.

3 At a fork of grassy tracks by an *Askrigg 5¼ miles, Carperby 1½ miles* signpost go through the bridlegate and take the right-hand of the two tracks (in other words, **not** alongside the wall on the left). At the next 3-way signpost bear **R** signposted *Askrigg 5*. At a X-roads with a broad stone track (GR 005 907) continue **SA** through a gate signposted *Askrigg*.

4 A good gravel track starts at the end of mining spoil heaps to the right. After 650m, at a *Bridleway to Askrigg & Woodhall* signpost (GR 978 905) turn **L** downhill through a gate then immediately **R** on a climbing stone track by a 3-way *Bridleway to Askrigg* signpost.

5 Continue west-north-west on this track for 3km. At the T-junction with the road turn **R** and climb for 2.4km to the summit.

6 Descend for 2.5km. **Ignore** the first broad stone track to the right. Shortly after the second farm drive to the left, just before the first trees, turn sharp **R** uphill on a broad stone track signposted *Bridleway to Castle Bolton* (GR 983 964).

7 Steady climb. After 1.8km **ignore** a wide track to the left (running parallel with the valley). Stay on the steeper right-hand track. The summit comes 3.5km after leaving the road.

8 Go past a rough old railway wagon shelter on a superb fast downhill. About 3.5km after the summit, at the offset crossroads of bridleways by a 4-way signpost and a grey metal barn (GR 030 942) turn **R** to go past an isolated house and climb the hill.

9 After reaching the summit, the next 3km back to the start are mainly downhill on a variety of surfaces: stone/grass/reeds/loose stone. At the bottom turn **R** to go past the castle to return to the car park.

←◎◎ Making a day of it

All or part of the *Apedale* section is also used in the two rides that go south from *Reeth – see pages 79 & 85*. The *Thornton Rust Moor* ride goes through Carperby – *see page 97* – and two rides start from *Bainbridge – see pages 109 & 127* – close to this ride at the Askrigg end (its southwest corner).

SWOOPING THROUGH THE BUTTERCUPS

Askrigg & Thornton Rust Moor

22.5km

Introduction

It was the middle of a beautiful summer's day. The sky went dark – an apocalyptic sort of dark. Then it began. The storm. I was high up on the moor with nowhere to hide. Thunder and lightning exploded and crashed just metres away from me. Rain? It wasn't rain, it was a fire hose directed straight at me by a prankster from hell. So what did I do? I sort of ducked and carried on, as though being six inches shorter would somehow stop me from being killed. So please excuse me if my memories of this ride are a bit distorted. I am sure the views of Wensleydale and Addlebrough were the stuff of dreams, that there was an excellent descent to Cubeck after the tour of Addlebrough and that Askrigg is a charming village with great pubs and tearooms. Let me know.

The Ride

Climb steeply out of Askrigg on picturesque Dales lanes to reach the start of the off-road – a wide stone track turning to rough grass after the barns at Heugh. Descend then contour below Ponderledge Scar to drop into Carperby and your only chance of a beer on the route. The footbridge over the River Swale is a convenient way of cutting out a section of the A684. (Cutting out is what the vegetation needs on the track climbing southwest from Throstle Gate up the Thornton Rust road!) The climb continues up onto the moorland. If the trail is at times indistinct, head towards the sharp left-hand outline of Addlebrough and the farm at Carpley Green. Briefly join tarmac before returning off-road, now on the north side of Addlebrough and on grassy tracks turning to stone before dropping back down to the start.

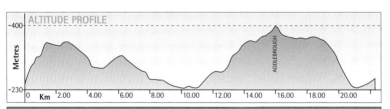

ALTITUDE PROFILE

Metres

-400

-230

0 Km 2.00 4.00 6.00 8.00 10.00 12.00 14.00 16.00 18.00 20.00

ADDLEBROUGH

ASKRIGG & THORNTON RUST MOOR

GRADE: ▲

DISTANCE: 22.5KM

TOTAL ASCENT: 520M

START/FINISH: ASKRIGG

GRID REFERENCE: 952 912

PARKING: FREE CAR PARK ON THE EASTERN EDGE OF VILLAGE.

CAFÉ: LOTS OF CHOICE IN ASKRIGG

PUBLIC HOUSE: LOTS OF CHOICE IN ASKRIGG. WHEATSHEAF, CARPERBY Tel: 01969 663 216

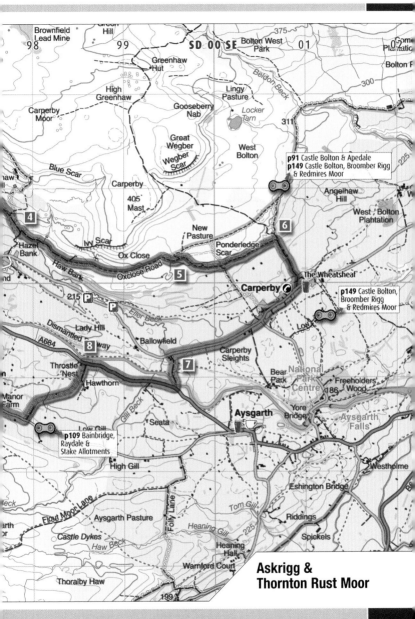

Askrigg &
Thornton Rust Moor

Directions – Askrigg &
Thornton Rust Moor

➲ With your back to the Crown Inn in Askrigg turn **L** then **L** again signposted *Muker*. Climb steeply for 800m and take the first road to the **R** signposted *Reeth*.

2 Shortly after a right-hand bend, at a fork of roads bear **L** on the upper lane. A second steep section. Take the first wide stone track to the **R** signposted *Bridleway to Castle Bolton* (GR 953 922).

3 After 1km **ignore** a road to the right. The stone track turns to a grassy tractor track after the barn by a *Bridal Way* (sic) sign. One reedy section. Go past a dilapidated corrugated iron barn. Parts of this stretch will be muddy in winter.

4 As the track swings sharp right downhill towards a cluster of buildings in Woodhall (GR 978 905) bear **L** through a gate in the wall to your left to continue in the same direction along an enclosed (walled) track. Pass through lead mining spoils following the direction of the signpost along a firm, smooth grass track and beneath a mast up to the left.

5 Go through a gate with a *Farm boundary - please keep gate closed* sign and immediately bear **R** parallel with the wall on the right. Follow this main track round to the **L**, passing a *Private* sign on a gate. At a path junction (GR 001 902) bear **L** to continue contouring parallel to the valley to your right.

6 At a T-junction with a broad stone track (GR 007 905) turn **R**. The track turns to tarmac. Keep bearing **R** through the village of Carperby. At the T-junction with the main road (Redmire to Askrigg) through the village turn **R** and go past the Wheatsheaf pub.

7 At the end of the village **ignore** a road to the left to Aysgarth Falls. After 1.5km take the next road to the **L** signposted *Aysgarth via footbridge*. Cross the footbridge then at the main road (A684) turn **R**.

8 After 1km take the first lane to the **L** immediately before a cluster of buildings (Throstle Nest). **Very easy to miss:** climb for 200m then, with the next farm (Hawthorn) in sight, as the tarmac turns to track at the end of the wall on the right, turn **R** onto a narrow overgrown track alongside a wall (GR 985 890).

9 After 1km, at the T-junction with the road turn **R**. In the village of Thornton Rust turn **L** opposite the Institute onto a lane signposted *Free car park*. Shortly, bear **L** at a fork, staying on the major track.

10 After about 1km and soon after crossing a stream, at the corner of the wall, turn **L** off the main track by a *Bridleway* sign (GR 967 884). Follow the obvious grassy track towards the left-hand end of the distinctive hill ahead (Addlebrough).

11 Climb then undulate, passing through a gate in the wall to the right and continuing towards Carpley Green Farm. At the road by the farm turn **R**.

12 **Easy to miss:** after 1.5km turn **R** off the lane by a *Bridleway to Cubeck* sign through an unusual combination of metal gate and half gate. Follow this contouring track east-northeast for 1.5km.

13 Shortly after going through a small, improved field of pasture turn **L** downhill by farm ruins (GR 949 890). At the road bear **L** steeply downhill.

14 At the main road (A684) turn **R** then **L** signposted *16.5 ton weight limit*. Shortly turn **R** at a road junction, cross the bridge over the River Ure and climb. At the T-junction turn **L** to return to the start in Askrigg.

◄◎◎ Making a day of it

The *Castle Bolton & Apedale* ride passes just north of Askrigg – *see page 91*. Two rides start from *Bainbridge* – *see pages 109 & 127* – and when you get to Carperby you are only 3km from the *Thoralby & Melmerby* ride – *see page 115*.

RATTLING INTO BURTERSETT

Hawes, a tour of
Dodd Fell & Burtersett

21km

Introduction

Climbing 300m on the Pennine Way south of Hawes up towards Dodd Fell is more of a walk than a ride but is still a better alternative to the unclassified road to the west (see *Warning* below). It leads to a fine track high above the vast bowl of Snaizeholme to the west. The route joins tarmac and turns northeast on the old Roman road known as Cam High Road. The fast descent along the whole length of the Roman road is covered in another ride, here the challenge is of a different, more technical nature as you drop steeply down to Burtersett.

The Ride

A wiggly lane route south through Hawes and Gayle takes you to the start of a steep grassy climb on the Pennine Way. You won't be spending much time in the saddle until the summit, but from there on, the trail is a gem, perched on the edge of the exceedingly steep hillside. Briefly join the road from Langstrothdale towards Hawes then dive off-road to the top of the 300m descent to Burtersett on a track which will test you and have you cursing the damage done by scramble bikes that keep trashing it despite the *No motorbikes* signs. A short sprint on the A684 returns you to Hawes.

Warning: *A right of way is marked on the map heading southwest off the B6255 Hawes to Ingleton road (starting at GR 859 896) which looks an ever so tempting alternative to the Pennine Way south of Hawes. Don't bother! What starts off as a broad stone-based track becomes a horrible steep, rubblefield where carrying your bike over ankle-twisting terrain is your only option.*

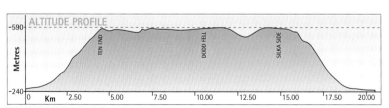

HAWES, A TOUR OF DODD FELL & BURTERSETT   GRADE: ▲

DISTANCE: 21KM

TOTAL ASCENT: 522M

START/FINISH: THE CENTRE OF HAWES

GRID REFERENCE: 872 899

PARKING: SEVERAL PAY & DISPLAY CAR PARKS IN HAWES

CAFÉ: LOTS OF CHOICE IN HAWES

PUBLIC HOUSE: LOTS OF CHOICE IN HAWES

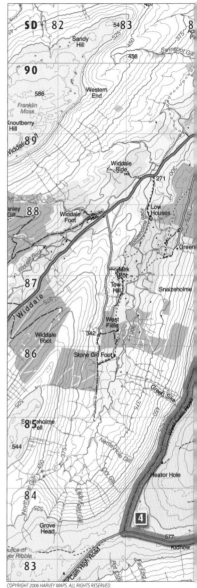

Hawes, a tour of
Dodd Fell & Burtersett

Directions – Hawes, a tour of Dodd Fell & Burtersett

5 From the centre of Hawes follow the A684 towards Sedbergh then shortly turn **L** signposted *Hayle, Kettlewell, Wensleydale Cheese Centre*. After 700m, in Gayle, on a sharp left-hand bend just before a *Weak Bridge* sign turn **R** by a letter box in the wall. Follow this road past houses to a T-junction by a small two-storey barn and turn **R**.

2 Shortly, at the next T-junction (GR 865 892), turn **L** uphill signposted *Gaudy House Farm* and soon turn **R** signposted *Pennine Way*. After 650m, at the farm gate, turn **L** into the field signposted *Pennine Way* and follow the wall on your right.

3 Climb on the Pennine Way on a rough path for almost 3km. At the junction with a better track bear **L**.

4 After 4km, at the junction with the road turn **L**.

5 After 3.5km, at a T-junction with a more major road bear **L** signposted *Hawes* then after 800m and shortly after a *Road narrows* road sign bear **R** onto a broad track signposted *Byway to Bainbridge*.

6 After 1.6km, **ignore** the first *Bridleway* sign to the left before the summit of the hill to the left. After a further 1km and about 20m **before** the gate across the main track turn L through a blue metal gate (GR 882 870) into the field signposted *Bridleway* (the post is in the corner of the field).

7 The grass track becomes grass and stone, occasionally rubble. Go past the farm. At the tarmac in the village of Burtersett turn **R** then **L**. Descend to the A684 and turn **L** to return to the start.

◄▭▭ Making a day of it

Another ride starts from Hawes heading northwest up onto *Lady Ann Clifford's Highway* across Mallerstang Common – *see page 135*. Two short rides start from *Hardraw*, just north of Hawes – *see page 19* – and two more from *Bainbridge*, a few kilometres to the east – *see pages 109 & 127*.

STRAIGHT-LINING IT FOR STALLING BUSK

Bainbridge, Raydale & Stake Allotments

26km

Introduction

Lying to the southwest of Bainbridge, Raydale has the feel of a forgotten valley and is surrounded by much bigger neighbours such as Wensleydale, Langstrothdale and Wharfedale. But this gives an old world charm to the hamlets of Countersett, Marsett and Stalling Busk, forming a triangle around Semer Water, the central feature of the valley. The cobbled crossing of Crooks Beck is one of the memorable challenges of the day. This is followed by a steep climb onto Stake Allotments which marks the start of totally different sort of ride: a faint track gently descending over a vast grassy plateau eventually turning to stone as it drops towards Thoralby.

The Ride

Climb out of Bainbridge on tarmac through the hamlet of Countersett to Marsett. The first off-road section brings you to a surprisingly long cobbled ford which can be 'interesting' after heavy rain. Make it across and face the steep loose climb to Stalling Busk. The tearoom might be open at the jam factory! More climbing takes you onto the plateau of Stake Allotments and onto a faint trail leading east off the main track. At times you just have to keep faith that you're on the right track as the trail flickers on and off. Keep on pointing east-north-east and you'll drop towards Thoralby. Drag yourself away from that fast stone descent to cut north across Haw Beck, thus avoiding a steep climb and a section of main road.

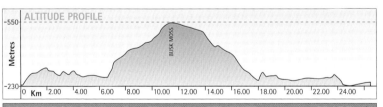

ALTITUDE PROFILE

Metres

-550

-230

0 Km | 2.00 | 4.00 | 6.00 | 8.00 | 10.00 | 12.00 | 14.00 | 16.00 | 18.00 | 20.00 | 22.00 | 24.00

BUSK MOSS

BAINBRIDGE, RAYDALE & STAKE ALLOTMENTS   GRADE: ▲

DISTANCE: 26KM

START/FINISH: BAINBRIDGE, ON THE A684 EAST OF HAWES

PARKING: VILLAGE GREEN, BAINBRIDGE

CAFÉ: CORN MILL TEAROOM, BAINBRIDGE Tel: 01969 650 212
OPEN EASTER TO OCTOBER

TOTAL ASCENT: 655M

GRID REFERENCE: 935 901

PUBLIC HOUSE: ROSE & CROWN, BAINBRIDGE
Tel: 01969 650 225

Bainbridge, Raydale & Stake Allotments

Directions – Bainbridge, Raydale & Stake Allotments

➡ From Bainbridge village green, opposite the Post Office, take the lane heading south-west signposted *Countersett, Semer Water, Marsett*. Shortly at a T-junction turn **L**.

2 After 3.5km go through the village of Countersett **ignoring** a right and a left turn.

3 After a further 2.5km, in the hamlet of Marsett, cross the bridge over Marsett Beck and turn immediately **L** onto a grassy track, soon joining a better stone track parallel with the river. Cross the footbridge or the cobbled ford.

4 The track is loose and rocky as it climbs up to the village of Stalling Busk. Turn **R** by the telephone box and climb steeply, taking the **second** broad stone track on the **R** signposted *Byway, Kidstones*.

5 Climb on a very fine track for 3.5km. Take the first major stone track to the **L** near a 2-way *Stalling Busk, Kidstones* signpost which points along the track you are leaving.

6 **Very easy to miss:** after 1km and shortly after the summit keep an eye out for a grassy track with vehicle marks bearing off to the **R**, passing to the **R** of the cairn on the horizon (GR 938 847).

7 Generally glorious gentle grassy descent over the next 5km, dropping 300m, although the route is occasionally vague. Aim east-north-east towards the sharp left-hand 'nose' of the hills ahead.

8 **Easy to miss:** join a better stone-based track and continue descending. On a sharp right-hand bend by a large ash and sycamore tree (GR 995 868) turn sharp **L** steeply uphill (the first 10m of the track are concrete). This turn comes 50m **before** the main track turns sharp left, so if you turn sharp right then sharp left you have gone too far.

9 At the fork at the top of a short steep climb bear **R** signposted *Bridleway*. Follow the direction of the finger post **exactly** towards the far left-hand corner of the field, not the more obvious track alongside the wall on the right. You will come to a distinctive yellow-topped signpost by a wooden bridlegate. Cross a small stream, followed by a short steep climb then a gentle descent on a walled grassy track.

10 At the T-junction with a major gravel track turn **R** then at the T-junction with a tarmac lane turn **L**.

11 After 2.5km go through the village of Thornton Rust. After a further 2km at the T-junction with the A684 turn **L** back to Bainbridge.

← Making a day of it

Another ride starts from *Bainbridge* going south to *Langstrothdale* – *see page 127*. A ride starts at *Thoralby* and heads east to West Burton, Carlton and *Melmerby* – *see page 115*. Two other rides start in or pass near Askrigg – *see pages 91 & 97*.

TOM MODELLING A NIFTY LITTLE RED NUMBER

Thoralby, West Burton, Carlton Moor & Melmerby

22km

Introduction

A quick look at the map shows a glaring lack of rides to the east of the B6160 (Grassington to Aysgarth road) and to the south of the A684. This is partly because of a scarcity of bridleways and partly because many of the legal tracks that do exist are either dead-ends or too boggy or too overgrown. So... make the most of this short tough circuit with its extremely challenging climb to the summit of Burton Moor/Carlton Moor. The descent gets better and better as you approach the pub opportunity in Carlton. A much easier tarmac climb sets you up for the final off-road: 5km of fun with the most exciting stuff on the descent towards West Burton.

The Ride

Nip across from one valley to the next: from Thoralby and Bishopdale Beck to West Burton and Walden Beck. The 300m climb from Cote to the summit is tough with lots of loose stone. Gaining the summit brings no immediate joy as the soft, peaty surface is often ripped up by scramble bikes and is hard work in winter, but it soon improves with 200m of descent on an ever more defined track. Recover on tarmac as you make your way through Carlton (pub) and Melmerby (no pub). Climb to the top with views west to the whaleback of the Height of Hazely and whizz downhill. Don't miss the turn off onto High Lane, a broad track that climbs gently then drops to Thoralby.

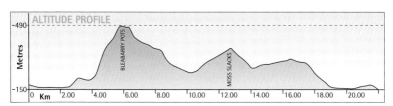

THORALBY, WEST BURTON, CARLTON MOOR & MELMERBY   GRADE: ▲

DISTANCE: 22KM

TOTAL ASCENT: 595M

START/FINISH: THORALBY, SOUTH OF AYSGARTH, OFF THE A684   **GRID REFERENCE:** 000 868

PARKING: IN THORALBY, JUST BEYOND THE GEORGE INN, AT THE BACK OF THE VILLAGE HALL, SIGNPOSTED *DAYTIME PARKING FOR VISITORS*   **CAFÉ:** BRING SANDWICHES

PUBLIC HOUSE: GEORGE INN, THORALBY Tel: 01969 663 256. FOX & HOUNDS, WEST BURTON Tel: 01969 663 111. FORESTERS ARMS, CARLTON Tel: 01969 640 272

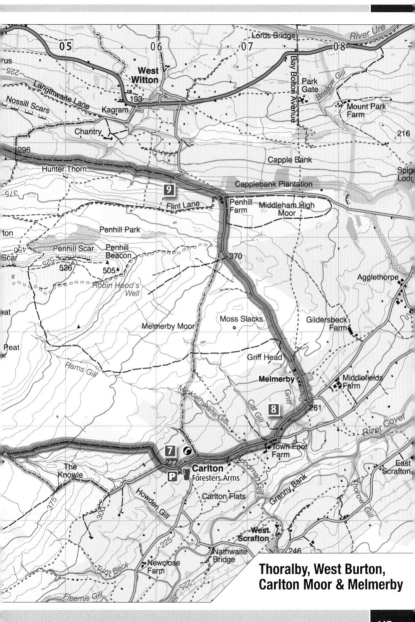

Thoralby, West Burton, Carlton Moor & Melmerby

Directions – Thoralby, West Burton, Carlton Moor & Melmerby

⑤▸ Exit the car park behind the village hall in Thoralby and aim for Thoralby Post Office/ village stores. **Easy to miss:** about 100m after the shop, at the end of the row of cottages on the right, turn **R** onto a narrow lane between the houses and a barn.

2 Cross the stream (Bishopdale Beck) via footbridge/ford. At the minor lane bear **L** then shortly at a T-junction with the B6160 bear **L** again.

3 After 1.5km on a left-hand bend turn sharp **R** signposted *West Burton*. At the top end of the 'green' in West Burton, go past the telephone box and bear **L** signposted *Walden only* onto a no through road. Climb and follow the road to the **L** signposted *Walden South*.

4 Cross a bridge over Walden Beck, go past Cote Farm then immediately bear **L** uphill alongside a wall to the left (in other words, **not** through the white gate), soon passing the tall square chimney of the former Braithwaite Lead Smelt Mill.

5 Very steep climb on broad rubbly path. Stay on the main path, **ignoring** a track to the right with a *Private road* sign.

6 The area either side of the summit has been badly cut up by scramble bikes but soon becomes a good grass and gravel track. Basically stay on the main track bearing **R** and passing through a gate with a *Bull in field* sign.

7 At the road turn **L** (GR 061 846). At the T-junction in Carlton turn **L**.

8 Go through the village and take the first road to the **L** signposted *Melmerby, Wensley*. Shortly, at the start of Melmerby, take the first road to the **L** signposted *West Witton*.

9 Climb to the summit and descend, following the road to the **L** signposted *West Witton*. **Easy to miss:** on a fast descent, shortly after a *1 in 4 hill* sign and just before a sharp right-hand hairpin bend, bear **L** onto a broad stone track (GR 062 877).

10 Climb then go gently downhill. Bear **R** at a fork of tracks where a footpath to *West Burton via Hudson Quarry* is signposted to the left. Fine descent to join tarmac, cross a bridge over Walden Beck and at the T-junction with the B6160 (at the edge of West Burton) turn sharp **R**.

11 Take the first road to the **L** signposted *Aysgarth, Hawes* then after 800m on a right-hand bend immediately after crossing Bishopdale Beck turn **L** onto a very narrow lane. After 1.5km bear **L** into Thoralby.

◄◯◯ Making a day of it

The ride from *Bainbridge* goes south into Raydale then east over Stake Allotments and passes just west of Thoralby – *see page 109*. The ride east from *Askrigg* can be joined in Carperby – *see page 97*. The start of the *Horsehouse to Scar House Reservoir* ride is 4km south west of Carlton – see this book's companion volume – *Yorkshire Dales Mountain Biking – The South Dales*.

SECTION 3

Enduros

Now we're talking. Pack your sarnies and your chain lube. These are big, tough rides (for big, tough riders?) that'll probably take you all day. They're challenging routes for fit and experienced mountain bikers – you know – proper riding.

Riding where you might describe the route as 'a bit of a beast'.

Enduros
sponsored by

FROM DARKNESS INTO LIGHT
LUMICYCLE

www.lumicycle.com

FAST AND HARD (EASY)

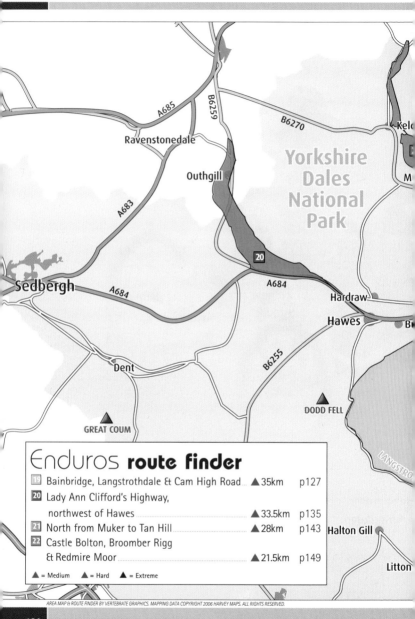

Enduros **route finder**

▲ = Medium   ▲ = Hard   ▲ = Extreme

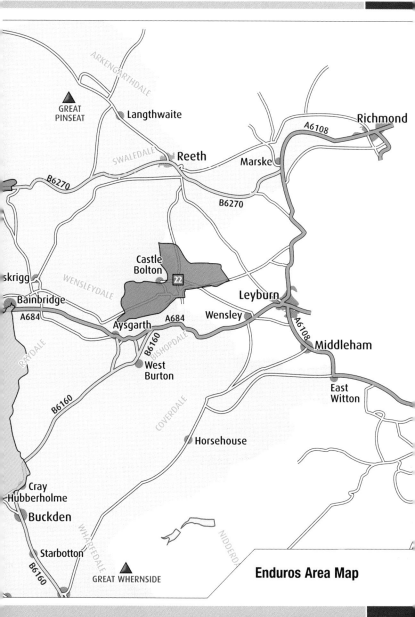

Enduros Area Map

WET CONDITIONS IN BISHOPDALE

Bainbridge, Langstrothdale & Cam High Road

35km

Introduction

A big, breezy, roof-of-the-world ride, twice climbing to over 550m on fine stone tracks, linked by a beautiful lane past two excellent pubs and through the gentle delights of Langstrothdale. For a long ride this can be done quite quickly as there is only one short section where the going is rough – especially true during the winter months. Then again, if you are in no hurry, it may be a ride where the call of the pub is such that you could spin it out to a full day.

The Ride

Leaving Bainbridge, follow a lane for 4km, climbing to Carpley Green Farm with views over archetypal Dales countryside. After an initial period of smooth stone, the track turns rougher and rutted, but smoothens as you approach the plateau. Bleak, innit? There are dramatic views on the descent towards Buckden Pike with one steep stone section to tackle. Zip down to tarmac, dropping to the White Lion at Cray and then the George Inn at Hubberholme. At 588m, the road between Langstrothdale and Hawes is the highest road pass in the Dales. A gentle climb off-road on Cam High Road and you are set for one of the fastest descents in the area, dropping 300m over 6km on the way back to Bainbridge.

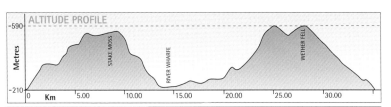

ALTITUDE PROFILE

Metres

STAKE MOSS

RIVER WHARFE

WETHER FELL

-590

-210

0   Km   5.00   10.00   15.00   20.00   25.00   30.00

BAINBRIDGE, LANGSTROTHDALE & CAM HIGH ROAD   GRADE: ▲

DISTANCE: 35KM

TOTAL ASCENT: 945M

START/FINISH: BAINBRIDGE, ON THE A684 EAST OF HAWES

GRID REFERENCE: 935 901

PARKING: AROUND THE GREEN IN BAINBRIDGE

CAFÉ: CORN MILL TEAROOM, BAINBRIDGE Tel: 01969 650 212 – OPEN EASTER TO OCTOBER

PUBLIC HOUSE: ROSE & CROWN, BAINBRIDGE Tel: 01969 650 225. WHITE LION, CRAY Tel: 01756 760 262.
GEORGE INN, HUBBERHOLME Tel: 01756 760 223

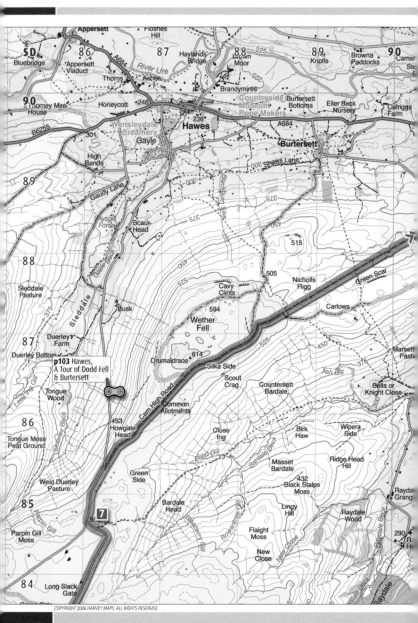

continues on
NEXT PAGE

**Bainbridge, Langstrothdale
& Cam High Road**

continued from PREVIOUS PAGE

3

4

5

Bainbridge, Langstrothdale & Cam High Road

Directions – Bainbridge, Langstrothdale & Cam High Road

➡ From the centre of Bainbridge follow the A684 towards Aysgarth and Leyburn. Cross the bridge, climb steeply and take the first lane to the **R** signposted *Semer Water, Stalling Busk*. After 800m **ignore** the first left to Scar Top (private road). Shortly, on a sharp right-hand bend take the next **L** signposted *Carpley Green* to climb past a mast.

2 Follow the tarmac to the end, go through Carpley Green Farm and onto a track signposted *Byway, Stake Road*. This is an excellent smooth stone track at the start. After one steep rock and rubble section it is mainly rideable on grassy tracks cut up a bit by vehicles.

3 About 4km after the farm, at the T-junction with a better stone track turn **L** signposted *Byway, Kidstones*. Follow this roof-of-the-world track with good smooth grassy sections.

4 More dramatic views on the fast descent. After a further 4km, at the road turn **R** for a fast tarmac descent.

5 Go past the White Lion pub in Cray then after 600m take the first lane to the **R** signposted *6ft 6ins width limit*. Shortly, at a T-junction turn **R** over the bridge (no sign). At the T-junction after the church and the bridge in Hubberholme turn **R** (no sign). Go past the George Inn.

6 Follow the beautiful lane for 11km towards Hawes, along the gentle wooded landscape of Langstrothdale then climbing steeply after Oughtershaw to the summit.

7 Shortly after the summit, go round a sharp left-hand then right-hand bend. Immediately after a *Road narrows* sign bear **R** onto a broad stone track signposted *Byway to Bainbridge*.

8 Short climb then long descent on wonderful Cam High Road, an old Roman road, for 8km. At the crossroads with a lane continue **SA** on a track signposted *Byway to Bainbridge*. After 2km join tarmac, bearing **L** downhill to return to Bainbridge.

◀ ⫘ Making a day of it

Another ride starts from *Bainbridge* heading east to *Thoralby* – *see page 109*. Two other rides start in or pass near *Askrigg* – *see pages 91 & 97*.

LADY ANN CLIFFORD'S HIGHWAY

Lady Ann Clifford's Highway, northwest of **Hawes**

33.5km

Introduction

One of the finest stretches of plateau cruising in the Dales, with views to Mallerstang, Baugh Fell and Wild Boar Fell, comes at a cost of 30 minutes hard slog where you may well feel tempted to say 'What's the point?' I certainly did. Don't worry – it is more than amply rewarded! There is an extraordinary stone sculpture on the top section called Water Cut by Mary Bourne. Down below are viaducts carrying the Settle–Carlisle railway, a conifer plantation and isolated farmhouses. It is, unfortunately, a tarmac return as there are no decent off-road alternatives. You could always use the same route for the return. If you do take the road, there's the chance of a beer in the Moorcock Inn near Garsdale Station.

The Ride

The start of this ride is rough, tough and reedy with a steep push up onto Cotter End. Passing the ruin of an old limestone kiln marks the start of the more enjoyable section. You are up at 500m, the views back down Wensleydale are staggering and ahead lies 10km of off-road cruising. At the beginning occasional tricky sections test your skills around stones on narrow bits or a quick spin of the pedals on short climbs after stream crossings but most of it is an easy reward for your earlier exertions. Stop and admire the stone sculpture as they must have spent a while choosing the right location for something so atmospheric. The descent to the road has its expected thrills, and then it's either a return along the same route or tarmac back to the start.

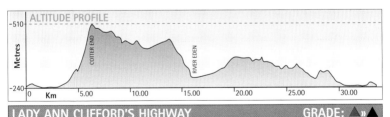

LADY ANN CLIFFORD'S HIGHWAY   GRADE: ▲»▲

GRADE: ▲ (WITH ONE ▲ 2KM SECTION AT THE START)   **DISTANCE:** 33.5KM

START/FINISH: HAWES   **TOTAL ASCENT:** 737M

PARKING: SEVERAL PAY & DISPLAY CAR PARKS IN HAWES   **CAFE:** LOTS OF CHOICE IN HAWES

PUBLIC HOUSE: MOORCOCK INN, GARSDALE HEAD Tel: 01969 667 488, LOTS OF CHOICE IN HAWES

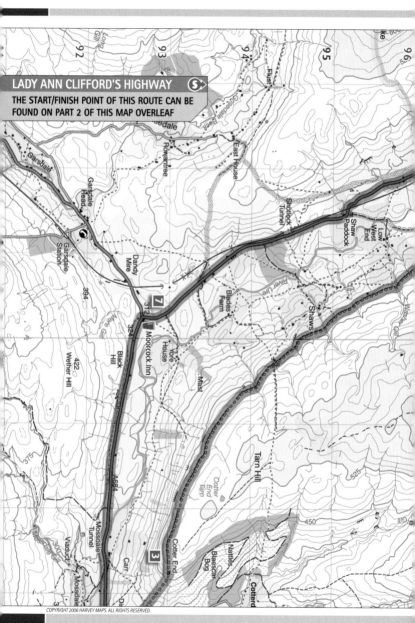

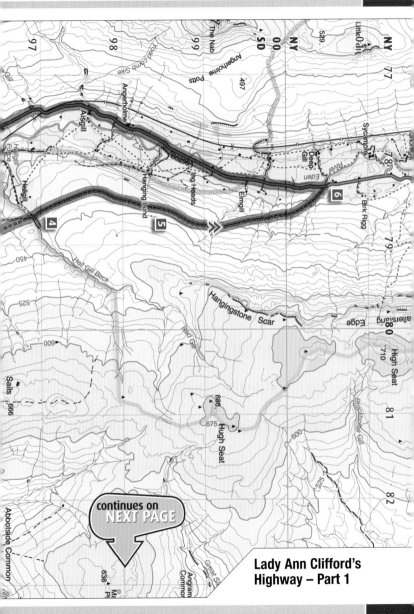

continues on
NEXT PAGE

**Lady Ann Clifford's
Highway – Part 1**

PHOTO: NICK COTTON

PHOTO: NICK COTTON

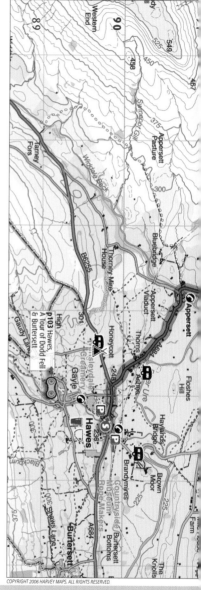

p103 Hawes,
A Tour of Dodd Fell
& Burtersett

continued from
PREVIOUS PAGE

**Lady Ann Clifford's
Highway – Part 2**

LADY ANN CLIFFORD'S HIGHWAY, NORTHWEST OF HAWES – GRADE ▲»▲

139

Directions – Lady Ann Clifford's Highway, northwest of Hawes

➎ Follow the A684 west from Hawes for 5km, **ignoring** the first road to the right to Hardraw.

2 Take the next lane to the **R** after 2km signposted *Cotterdale only* (opposite Collier Holme Farm, GR 842 921) then turn **L** immediately through the bridlegate onto the rough track signposted *Lady Ann Clifford's Highway*, running at first parallel with the main road. The next 2km are a tough, reedy push along the level then steeply up following a line of posts. Parts have been trashed by scramble bikes. It *will* be worth it, honest!

3 Go through a bridlegate up past a large round limestone kiln and up to the highpoint. After a superb, open and airy 2km section on a broad, smooth stone and grass track (with the occasional bit of limestone technical) the improved stone track starts. Go past a couple of ruins.

4 After 4km on this newly improved track, cross the solid stone Hell Gill Bridge. After the bridge the route runs along an ever better smooth stone grass track and limestone pavement.

5 About 1.7km after the bridge you arrive at a dramatic stone sculpture – *Water Cut* by Mary Bourne. About 2km after the sculpture join the road after a superb descent with the occasional square stone water channel (**beware**!).

6 At the B6259 turn sharp **L** and follow it for 9km.

7 At the T-junction with the A684 by the Moorcock Inn turn **L** signposted *Hawes* for a further 10km to return to the starting point.

Public Path
Lady Ann's Way

◄⚙⚙⚙ Making a day of it

Another ride starts from *Hawes* heading around *Dodd Fell* – *see page 103*. The two short rides from *Hardraw* exploring *Abbotside Common* and *Cotterdale* are also close by – *see page 19*.

COOLING OFF IN A FORD SOUTH OF KELD

North from **Muker** to **Tan Hill**

28km

Introduction

Keld and Muker are the first villages you find at the western end of Swaledale, linked in this ride by some contrasting bridleways. The first half of the ride stays along the east side of the River Swale, past old mining ruins at the junction of the Swale with Swinner Gill, then it climbs through woodland above the valley. In contrast, the return from Keld to Muker lies away from the valley, climbing steeply over Kisdon Hill with fantastic views from the top and a steep grassy descent. You can extend the ride north from Keld up to Tan Hill and the highest pub in England, returning via the Pennine Way. The going is very soft in winter, so this northern loop is only worth trying in the drier months of the year.

The Ride

After an easy section from Muker along the B6270 the route turns sharply uphill after the river. Tarmac becomes track, climbing gently past ruins, then steeply above the precipitous valley with great views below. In Keld you have the choice of a short ride, returning via Kisdon Hill or a longer option using the road to Tan Hill to gain height before dropping down on the grassy Pennine Way back to Keld. Watch your wheels near stream crossings on suddenly soft patches that grab your front wheel and catapult you skywards. Whichever route you choose, the tough climb up Kisdon Hill rewards you with views across the valley and a steep, grassy descent that saw me lose control big time in the wet, causing my bike and me to part company.

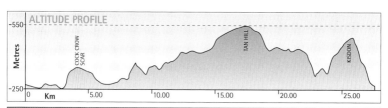

ALTITUDE PROFILE

NORTH FROM MUKER TO TAN HILL

GRADE: ▲

DISTANCE: 28KM

START/FINISH: MUKER, ON THE B6270 WEST OF REETH

PARKING: PAY & DISPLAY AT THE EAST END OF THE VILLAGE

PUBLIC HOUSE: TAN HILL INN (THE HIGHEST PUB IN ENGLAND) Tel: 01833 628 246.
FARMERS ARMS, MUKER Tel: 01748 886 297

CAFE: TEA SHOP & VILLAGE STORE, MUKER Tel: 01748 886 409

TOTAL ASCENT: 915M

GRID REFERENCE: 911 978

North from Muker to Tan Hill

Directions – North from Muker to Tan Hill

➌ From the car park in Muker follow the B6270 east towards Reeth.

2 **Easy to miss:** after 2.5km take the first lane to the **L**, sharply downhill, just after crossing a bridge over Oxnop Beck (no sign, GR 934 976). Cross the bridge over the River Swale, climb steeply past a telephone box, then at the brow of the hill turn **L** onto a no through road to continue steeply uphill.

3 After 1km at a fork of tarmac lanes, with a house nestling in the fork, bear **R** on the upper lane. After a further 1.5km at the next fork at the end of the tarmac section bear **R** on the upper track then follow the main stone track as it descends to the river.

4 Follow the track alongside the river, across the bridge over Swinner Gill then past the ruins. Climb steeply to the highpoint by a barn ruin.

5 Descend to cross a larger bridge over a stream. At the fork of tracks by a wooden bench beyond the bridge bear **R*** for the full route signposted *Pennine Way*.

* ▶**OR** for a short cut, turn **L** signposted *Keld* and rejoin at **9**.

6 Climb steeply, then at the fork of tracks beyond the gate bear **L** signposted *Bridleway* (the route to the right, the Pennine Way, is the return route). After 1.3km, at the T-junction with the road turn **R** steeply uphill.

7 Follow this road for almost 6km. At the T-junction turn **R**. Opposite the Tan Hill Inn turn **R** onto a track signposted *Pennine Way*. Keep following *Pennine Way* signs generally downhill. The going will be soft in winter – watch out for wheel traps.

8 Cross a stone bridge over Mould Gill (GR 888 037). Go past some barns and the track improves. **Easy to miss:** shortly after the barns, leave the main track as it goes uphill towards Frith Lodge and bear **R** by a *Pennine Way* signpost onto a grassy track. The track is a mixture of hard and soft.

9 Rejoin the outward route just east of Keld and continue downhill on the Pennine Way. Just before the bridge over East Gill (GR 896 011) turn sharp **R** downhill signposted *Keld*. Descend via steps to cross the bridge over the River Swale. Climb via more steps and bear **R**, leaving the Pennine Way. At the square in Keld turn **L** then soon fork **L** and at the junction with the B6270 turn **L** once more signposted *Reeth, Richmond*.

10 After 300m turn **L** downhill on a track by a triangle of grass signposted *Bridleway to Muker*. Steep 160m climb rewarded by great views. Fast grassy descent.

11 At a junction of tracks (GR 904 985) by a small barn turn **L** (the Pennine Way goes right). Descend on track then tarmac down to Muker.

← Making a day of it

NB A glance at the map reveals a tempting looking bridleway running southeast from Tan Hill towards Arkengarthdale. Unless you are a devotee of carrying your bike through bogs you would be well advised to avoid it. Coming from Arkengarthdale it is excellent as far as Punchard Coal Level (at GR 946 043).

Slip east down the valley to test the rides from *Gunnerside – see page 31* – and over *Reeth High Moor – see page 73* – which can themselves be linked together.

PHOTO: NICK COTTON

HEADING INTO APEDALE

Castle Bolton, Broomber Rigg & Redmire Moor

21.5km

Introduction

A castle, a tearoom, two pubs, a chance to go 'ooh!' and 'ahh!' at Aysgarth Waterfalls, strange signs for tanks on Redmire Moor, ghostly mining spoils and enough climbing to keep you fit. This is best left for a fine day in summer when the tracks are drier and the views over Wensleydale are at their best.

The Ride

Head west from Castle Bolton on a broad track through lots of gates and drop down on a sunken beauty to Carperby. If you are already in need of coffee, there are four cafés/tearooms around the pretty village of Aysgarth and at Aysgarth Falls, just off the route. The ride turns east through fields and woodland to Redmire and a steep climb up a mining road up into tank territory. Turn off tarmac and head west through the mining spoils on Redmire Moor. Jink right then left on tarmac to arrive at the well-loved bridleway crossroads at the bottom of the Apedale road. Up and over the hill, south to Castle Bolton with a final rubbly tooth-rattler to finish.

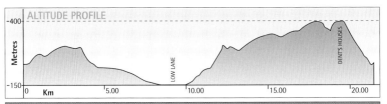

ALTITUDE PROFILE

Metres

-400

-150

0 | Km | 5.00 | 10.00 | 15.00 | 20.00

LOW LANE

DENT'S HOUSES

CASTLE BOLTON, BROOMBER RIGG & REDMIRE MOOR   GRADE: ▲

DISTANCE: 21.5KM

START/FINISH: CASTLE BOLTON

PARKING: BY BOLTON CASTLE

PUBLIC HOUSE: WHEATSHEAF, CARPERBY Tel: 01969 663 216

TOTAL ASCENT: 450M

GRID REFERENCE: 033 919

CAFÉ: CAFÉ AT BOLTON CASTLE

**Castle Bolton, Broomber
Rigg & Redmire Moor**

Directions – Castle Bolton, Broomber Rigg & Redmire Moor

➜ Exit the car park opposite Bolton Castle and turn **R** through the gate signposted *Askrigg*. Follow this broad smooth stone track through a whole series of gates. The waymarking is with yellow dots, arrows and yellow-tipped posts.

2 After 1.4km pass between barns and go through a gate onto a slightly rougher track with a wall to the left. After 400m follow the main track through a gate in the wall to the left, soon running through woodland parallel to the wall. After the next gate the track turns to grass and the wall is once again to the left.

3 At a fork of grassy tracks by a signpost *Askrigg 5¼ miles, Carperby 1½ miles* go through a bridlegate adjacent to a field gate and take the **RH** of two grassy tracks (i.e. **not** alongside wall to the left). At the next 3-way signpost bear **L** signposted *Carperby ¾*.

4 Descend on a sunken grassy track then at a T-junction with a better stone track turn **L** signposted *Carperby ½*. The track turns to tarmac. At the T-junction with the main Redmire to Askrigg road through Carperby turn **R** and go past the Wheatsheaf pub.

5 At the end of the village turn **L** signposted *Aysgarth Falls, National Park Centre* then shortly turn **L** again onto a no-through-road. Go past the farm

6 **Easy to miss.** Shortly after passing a round-roofed barn on the right and just beyond a small wooden hut on the left leave the tarmac and go through a wide field gate to the **L** descending on a grassy track past two wooden barns. Continue downhill beneath a railway bridge and into the woods on a narrow track. Track turns to tarmac at the farm.

7 At the road turn **R** to go through Redmire and past the Bolton Arms pub. Climb for 1km, passing beneath a railway bridge then take the second lane to the **L** signposted *Barracks* (GR 058 915).

8 Climb steeply, pass a quarry to the left. On a gentle descent, opposite a lane to Preston to the right, turn **L** uphill onto a wide stone track signposted *Unsuitable for motors.*

9 After 1.2km at a fork of tracks (GR 069 930) immediately after the cattle grid bear **L** on the lower track towards the chimney on the horizon. Follow this broad smooth stone track for 2.5km to the road and turn **R**.

10 After 800m, immediately after a cattlegrid, bear **L** onto a broad stone track signposted *Bridleway* by a *14% Gradient* road sign. At the bottom of the descent by a grey metal barn turn **L** (just before a 4-way signpost) to continue descending towards a deserted house.

11 After 1km as the main track swings right alongside the wall go **SA** through gates onto a wide grassy track between fences. The descent is on a variety of surfaces: stone/grass/reeds/loose stones. At the bottom turn **R** to go past the castle to return to the car park.

←⚙ Making a day of it

Another ride starts from *Castle Bolton* heading west and north exploring Apedale - *see page 91*. The *Thornton Rusk Moor* ride goes through Carperby - *see page 97*.

SECTION 4

Killers

Character building...

We wouldn't go so far as to say that these loops could kill you, but they won't be much fun if you're not prepared.

Hard climbs, hard descents and plenty of 'em.

Killers

sponsored by

www.shecycles.com

CRUISING ALONG GILBERT LANE

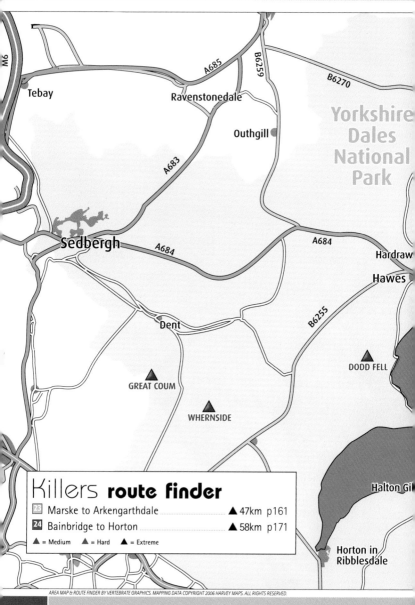

Killers **route finder**

▲ = Medium ▲ = Hard ▲ = Extreme

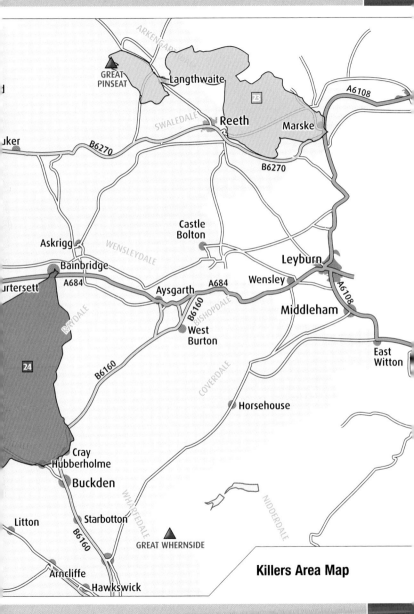

Killers Area Map

SKETCHY DESCENT FROM FREMINGTON EDGE

Marske to Arkengarthdale

47km

Introduction

Two longer rides are featured in the book which, as can be seen easily enough, are the amalgamation of shorter rides featured elsewhere, creating a longer and tougher challenge. This one starts in the northeast corner of the National Park from the small village of Marske and runs as far west as the mining tracks of Arkengarthdale up on Whaw Moor. The scenery becomes wilder the further north and west you go, climbing eventually to a 550m high-point on Great Pinseat. In between there is pasture and woodland, stretches alongside the lovely River Swale, steep climbs and wondrous descents, two fine pubs at Langthwaite and a long spell of high moorland cruising over Hurst Moor. Nuff said.

The Ride

A route of many turnings takes you from Marske to the River Swale and through fields to Marrick Abbey. Climb steeply from Fremington onto Fremington Edge and the first of three highpoints on the ride. The track over Marrick Moor to the tall chimney by Hall Farm is top quality, as is the downhill through the mining spoils to Langthwaite, once you've found it. The Whaw Moor loop will test legs and lungs as you climb up to 550m, the second highpoint. Enjoy the fruits of your labours on a fine descent to Langthwaite. A steep road climb then takes you towards the hamlet of Booze and onto Hurst Moor, the third highpoint, for the long run to Schoolmaster Pasture. The last few kilometres still have a few fireworks, notably the descent to Helwith Bridge and, after a last climb, a finale of almost 200m of descent to the finish. Whew!

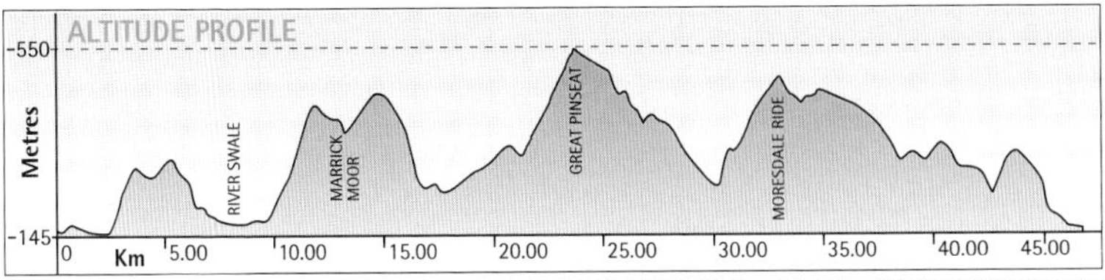

ALTITUDE PROFILE
550
145
Metres
Km
0
5.00
10.00
15.00
20.00
25.00
30.00
35.00
40.00
45.00
RIVER SWALE
MARRICK MOOR
GREAT PINSEAT
MORESDALE RIDE

MARSKE TO ARKENGARTHDALE — GRADE: ▲

DISTANCE: 47KM
TOTAL ASCENT: 1535M
START/FINISH: MARSKE, EAST OF REETH
GRID REFERENCE: 104 004
PARKING: PARKING NEAR THE BRIDGE OVER MARSKE BECK
CAFÉ: LOTS OF CHOICE JUST OFF THE ROUTE IN REETH
PUBLIC HOUSE: RED LION Tel: 01748 884 218, CB INN Tel: 01748 884 567, BOTH IN LANGTHWAITE. LOTS OF CHOICE JUST OFF THE ROUTE IN REETH

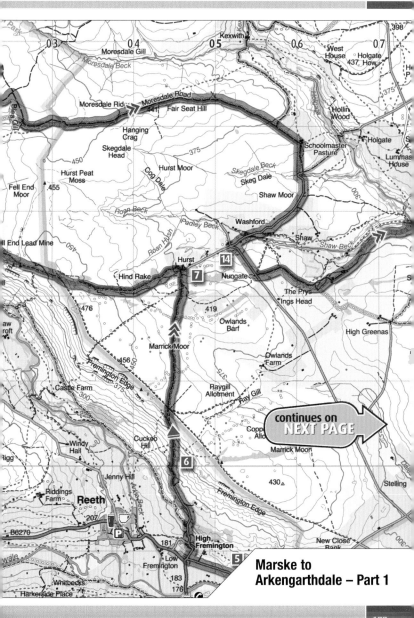

continues on
NEXT PAGE

**Marske to
Arkengarthdale – Part 1**

continued from
LAST PAGE

**Marske to
Arkengarthdale – Part 2**

Directions – Marske to Arkengarthdale

➡ From the car parking area in Marske (GR 104 004) follow the road south towards Leyburn and Richmond for almost 1.5km. **Easy to miss:** go past a large farm on the left (Bushy Park). On the descent, about 50m after an *Other Danger* road sign (!) and a *Road liable to subsidence* road sign turn sharp **R** through a gate onto a broad stone track (opposite the first *Road bumps* sign).

2 The track turns to tarmac. **Very easy to miss:** about 450m after the start of tarmac, on a climbing section, turn **R** onto a faint stone and grass track by a rounded wall end (there is a yellow dot on the wall). If you go past the farm at Low Oxque you have gone too far. Pass close to the barn (keep it to your right) on an overgrown track, go through a gate, soon bearing **L** towards a second gate leading into a steeply rising field. After 100m jink **L** then **R** through a bridlegate to join a better track with the fence now to your right.

3 After 650m at a 2-way *Bridleway* signpost turn **L** to continue uphill, keeping the fence to your right. After 1.5km bear **R** on the lower track (GR 091 986). After almost 1km pass to the **L** of the farm (Nun Cote Nook) then at the T-junction with the road turn **L** uphill. Descend into Marrick. **Ignore** a no through road to the left, then on a right-hand bend take the next lane to the **L** downhill opposite a partially-hidden telephone box. Shortly go round a right-hand bend then take the no through road to the **L** by a hay barn.

4 Follow the lane/track round to the **R** then immediately turn **L** down a walled grassy track signposted *No vehicular access* (GR 078 979). Soon join a broad stone and grass track. Go through a farm (Wood House) and join tarmac, going past Marrick Priory.

5 At the T-junction at the end of Marrick Priory road bear **L** for 700m. About 50m **before** the T-junction with the B6270 in Fremington turn **R** steeply uphill onto a narrow lane between a garage and houses. At the T-junction at the top of the climb turn **L** then follow the road round to the **R** to continue steeply uphill between a barn and a house in High Fremington.

6 Follow the steep tarmac lane to its end and onto a stone track. The gradient eases as you go through a gate in the boundary wall (GR 044 007). Superb track over Marrick Moor. At the T-junction with the road by a tall chimney turn **L** signposted *Bridleway* and go through a gate onto track.

7 Go past the grouse butts, climb to the summit then bear **L** towards the gate in the wall near the junction of walls, fence and path (GR 031 023). Great descent down through mining spoils. Go through a gate and continue downhill signposted *Langthwaite*. At the T-junction at the bottom by the buildings of Storthwaite Hall turn **R**. Cross the ford, climb then follow the main track parallel with the river.

8 At the T-junction by the Red Lion in Langthwaite turn **L**, cross the bridge over Arkle Beck then turn **R** on the road towards Tan Hill for 3.5 km, going past the church, the CB Inn and a right turn to Barnard Castle. **Ignore** the first bridleway to the left. Go past Moor Intake Farm up to the left and several houses and barns to the right. Take the next track to the **L** (GR 981 042) signposted *Bridleway only no vehicles* (a cluster of houses in the village of Whaw lies down in the valley to the right).

9 At a fork of tracks just before a round-roofed corrugated iron shed bear **L** to continue uphill and almost immediately bear **R** (in other words, do **not** go alongside the shed). Zig zag on the track passing above the spoil heap and climb steeply. The summit is marked by grassed-over spoil heaps. Turn sharp **L** at a T-junction of tracks (GR 975 030) towards a larger spoil heap, not grassed over. The track soon improves dramatically for a fine descent.

10 At the T-junction with the road turn **R** then, **easy to miss**, after 500m and shortly after a *1 in 5 gradient* sign before a steep right-hand bend, turn **L** uphill through a gate onto a broad grass and stone track signposted *Bridleway only, no vehicles*. Shortly, at a fork, bear **L** onto the wider, better defined path. Follow this for 2.2km to the T-junction with the road and turn **L** towards Langthwaite.

11 After 500m turn **R** to cross the bridge over Arkle Beck into Langthwaite village, go **SA** past the Red Lion pub and climb steeply. Shortly after the summit the tarmac ends. After 300m at the fork bear **L** on the upper track signposted *Fountain Farm*. **Easy to miss:** at the gate 100m before the farm turn **L** steeply uphill on a grassy track by a ruin. At the end of the rough, collapsed wall section bear **R** to go through a metal field gate and continue uphill.

12 After 300m, at the *Bridleway* sign, leave the main tractor track and bear **R** following the direction of the signpost alongside the wall to a gate near a small, low stone barn. Go steeply uphill on a faint track, soon turning **L** on a broad loose stone track then bearing **R** at fork of tracks by a wall corner to continue uphill towards a wooden post. At a T-junction with a better track on a hairpin bend bear **R** then shortly **R** again. Go past a low wooden building with a corrugated roof, continue climbing then at a fork of tracks after 800m bear **R** by a stone with *Hurst* written on it in white paint.

13 Great, easy descent over 5km, swooping down to a farmhouse (Schoolmaster Pasture). Continue descending, bear **R** at a T-junction to cross the bridge over Skegdale Beck and join tarmac, climbing the hill opposite. Climb, descend to cross Padley Beck, climb again. At the T-junction by a telephone box turn **L**. Climb steadily and take the first broad stone track to the **L** by a sign for *Prys House Farm, Bridleway*.

14 Go past the farm, through the farmyard and into a field with no obvious track. Follow the line of telegraph poles to a metal bridlegate in the wall ahead and continue through the next field alongside the wall to the left. Follow the zig zag track down to the river.

15 At the bottom of the descent but **before** the bridge, bear **R** steeply back up the hill on a loose stone track. Go over the summit and enjoy a great grassy downhill with views down into the Marske valley. At the road turn **R**. At the T-junction just above Marske turn **L** downhill to return to the start.

Bainbridge to Horton

58km

Introduction

Linking Wensleydale to Ribblesdale by way of Langstrothdale and Littondale, this long tough ride has five major climbs in the very heart of the National Park, one of which, from Raisgill over Horse Head Moor to Halton Gill is probably the toughest in the book. What goes up must come down and the hardest climbs seem to lead to the most satisfying descents, this particularly being the case for the mighty drop down into Littondale. Throw in some excellent pubs at Cray and Hubberholme, a fine pub AND café at Horton, the highest road pass in the Dales up over Oughtershaw Side and one of the fastest off-road descents in the Dales down Cam High Road, the old Roman road to Bainbridge, and you have a ride of superlatives.

The Ride

Leave Bainbridge and climb on tarmac to Carpley Green Farm with scenic views to the west over archetypal Dales countryside, in front of the sharp outline of Green Scar. After a smooth start the track turns rougher, but the going eases as you approach the plateau, with dramatic views on the rocky descent, towards Buckden Pike. Zip down the tarmac and drop into the wooded Langstrothdale. The gradient steepens at Cush Rigg and Oughtershaw as you climb out; at 588m, the road between Langstrothdale and Hawes is the highest road pass in the Dales. After a gentle climb off-road on Cam High Road you are set for one of the fastest descents in the area, dropping 300m over 8km on this straight and broad stone track, an old Roman road back to Bainbridge.

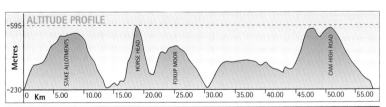

BAINBRIDGE TO HORTON

GRADE: ▲

DISTANCE: 58KM

START/FINISH: BAINBRIDGE, ON THE A684 EAST OF HAWES

PARKING: AROUND THE GREEN IN BAINBRIDGE

CAFÉ: THE PEN Y GHENT CAFE IN HORTON Tel: 01729 860 333, SHUT TUESDAYS

TOTAL ASCENT: 1655M

GRID REFERENCE: 935 901

PUBLIC HOUSE: BAINBRIDGE, CRAY, HUBBERHOLME, HORTON

continues on **NEXT PAGE**

Bainbridge to Horton – Part 1

continued from
PREVIOUS PAGE

**Bainbridge to Horton –
Part 2**

Directions – Bainbridge to Horton

➎ From the centre of Bainbridge follow the A684 towards Aysgarth and Leyburn. Cross the bridge and climb steeply, take the first lane to the **R** signposted *Semer Water, Stalling Busk*. After 800m **ignore** the first left to Scar Top (private road). Shortly, on a sharp right-hand bend take the next **L** signposted *Carpley Green* to climb past a mast.

2 Follow the tarmac to the end, go through Carpley Green Farm and onto a track signposted *Byway, Stake Road*. This is an excellent smooth stone track at the start. After one steep rock and rubble section it is mainly rideable on grassy tracks cut up a bit by vehicles. About 4km after the farm, at the T-junction with a better stone track turn **L** signposted *Byway, Kidstones*.

3 Roof-of-the-world track with good smooth grassy sections. More dramatic views on the fast descent. After a further 4km, at the road turn **R** for a fast tarmac descent.

4 Go past the White Lion pub in Cray then after 600m take the first lane to the **R** signposted *6ft 6ins width limit*. Shortly, at a T-junction turn **R** over the bridge (no sign). At the T-junction after the church and the bridge in Hubberholme turn **R** (no sign). Go past the George Inn.

5 After 2.5km, immediately after passing a cluster of buildings on the left at Raisgill, turn **L** by a stone and concrete cairn signposted *Halton Gill* (GR 905 786) off tarmac and onto track. The next 2.3 km are very steep, and largely unrideable up to the summit (350m of ascent). This is followed by an absolutely fabulous descent down into Littondale.

6 At the road at the bottom turn **R**. After 800m, and about 50m after the end of the tarmac, opposite the stone hump-backed bridge by Foxup Bridge Farm, turn **L** signposted *Bridleway to Horton in Ribblesdale*. At the gate that leads into a field with no obvious track bear **R** steeply uphill towards a gap in a stone wall and a wooden, blue-topped signpost (near a TV aerial). Go through a gate and continue in same direction.

7 Follow the direction of the signpost on a track parallel to the wall and at a distance of about 100m from it. After 800m it swings **R** on a more level course parallel with the ridge to the left. After 1.2km of relatively flat riding, at a gate in the stone wall and a signpost with *Bridleway to Horton 4¼ miles*, bear steeply **L** uphill following the direction of the signpost (GR 855 763).

8 Lots of fun tricky stone and grass to navigate. There is a short section of improved yellow gravel path which starts soon after a footpath to Plover Hill. The improved section ends and there is a rougher stretch of about 1.5km before the start of the descent on a broad stone track. At a fork turn **R** then at the road (B6479) turn **R** again through Horton. On a sharp left-hand bend turn **R** in front of the Crown Inn through the front car park onto the Pennine Way.

9 After 5km at a fork of tracks where the Pennine Way goes left bear **R**. Soon join a better forest track/road and bear **R**. Join tarmac by farm. Go through several gates over the next 5km. At the T-junction with the road turn **L**.

10 Follow the beautiful lane for 7km towards Hawes, climbing steeply after Oughter-shaw. Shortly after the summit, go round a sharp left-hand then right-hand bend. Immediately after a *Road narrows* sign bear **R** onto a broad stone track signposted *Byway to Bainbridge*.

11 Climb then descend on wonderful Cam High Road, an old Roman road, for 8km. At the crossroads with a lane continue **SA** on a track signposted *Byway to Bainbridge*. Join tarmac, bear **L** downhill to return to Bainbridge.

SECTION 5

Bonus Section

Top ten climbs –
clean them all, no dabs,
and you've earned yourself a cake.

Top ten descents –
reward enough in themselves!

Top ten cruises –
enjoy the view,
the feel of the wind in your hair...

This isn't even really a 'top' ten – such a small number of descents wouldn't do the Dales justice. It's more a selection of our favourites.

Sedbergh & the Howgills (Sedbergh and Howgill Summits) GR 671960

From the highest point of the Howgills across the undulating summits then down from Winder on grassy heaven.

Cam High Road to Burtersett (Hawes, Dodd Fell & Burtersett) GR 882870

A change from the smoother downhills. Hone your rock garden skills on this long, hard and rough descent from the old Roman Road to Burtersett.

Keld to Muker (Muker & Tan Hill) GR 896994

Massive views from the top of Kisdon Hill before an ever steeper grassy blast.

Return to Gunnerside (Gunnerside & Melbecks Moor) GR 963983

Short but testing mining track down off Low Row Pasture in the heart of Swaledale.

Reeth High Moor and Old Gang Smelting Mills (Reeth & Reeth High Moor) GR 964014

Long downhill cruise past the atmospheric ruins of the smelting mills.

Langthwaite, northwest of Reeth (Langthwaite & Hurst Moor) GR 031023

Switchbacks from Hurst Moor down through the spoils of Fell End lead mine to Storthwaite Hall in Arkengarthdale.

Marske (Marske & Marrick Moor) GR 084016

Fast and beautiful grass or grass & stone down off Skelton Moor in this little-known valley west of Marske.

West of Apedale Head down to the Askrigg road (Reeth & Apedale) GR 000954

The Apedale road could feature as best climb and best descent in either direction – a Dales classic.

Descent to Cray (Bainbridge & Langstrothdale) GR 938812

After some easy cruising over Stake Moss, get almost technical on this 180m downhill to the B6160 (two good pubs to come!)

Roman Road into Bainbridge (Bainbridge & Langstrothdale) GR 875866

It's long, it's fast and surprise, surprise it's straight. What did the Romans ever do for mountain biking?

FEEL THE BURN...

Always a difficult one to choose! The best climbs are not the steepest and roughest as these are pushes, (no one could ride from Bram Rigg Beck up to Bram Rigg Top on the Howgills), but those that are steep and testing enough to be just do-able without dabbing.

Hardraw, north of Hawes (Two Short Rides from Hardraw)   GR 867912
Northwest up the Pennine Way from the road in Hardraw. 260m climb.

Apedale – in both directions (Reeth & Apedale)   GR 982965 or GR 030942
The perfect Dales trail with good climbs and descents as you cross east to west or vice versa. 170m climb in each direction.

Stake Allotments (Bainbridge & Langstrothdale)   GR 943872
South of Carpley Green Farm onto Stake Allotments. 165m climb.

North of Muker (Muker & Tan Hill)   GR 909005
Following the crossing of Swinner Gill by the ruins in upper Swaledale. Only 100m ascent but a good test.

Whaw Moor, NW of Langthwaite (Langthwaite & Whaw Moor)   GR 975035
Zig zag up above the spoil heaps of Danby lead mines spoil heap. 220m climb.

Northwest of Marske onto Skelton Moor (Marske Beck)   GR 094013
Just the gradient to throw down a gauntlet. 150m climb.

Semer Water to Stake Moss (Bainbridge, Raydale & Stake Allotments) GR 919861
South on High Lane up to the vast plateau. 200m climb.

Four road climbs to make you wince!

Without any technical challenge to take your mind off the pain, road climbs hurt! Those listed below will test the fittest:

Gunnerside (Gunnerside & Melbecks Moor)   GR 953963
Push the button, the gate swings open and crawl up this 160m killer.

Langthwaite to Booze, NW of Reeth (Langthwaite & Hurst Moor) GR 005025
Only 100m up but the climb out of Langthwaite will test the strongest legs.

South of Grinton (Reeth & Apedale)   GR 046984
240m grunt of a climb on the Redmire road before the off-road fun begins.

Langstrothdale (Bainbridge & Langstrothdale)   GR 926782
Join the River Wharfe at Hubberholme and climb 350m to the highest road crossing through the Dales.

JUS' TRUCKIN' ON THRU

The best *specialités de la region* (or *de la* Dales) are the well-drained grassy summits and broad grouse moor tracks offering top grade cruising, normally the reward for some staggeringly unpleasant climbs.

Bram Rigg Top to Winder (Sedbergh & Howgill Summits)   GR 668967–655935

The biggest climb in the book gives one of best cruises in the UK. Leave for a day of crisp visibility – because you're worth it.

Lady Ann Clifford's Highway (from Hawes)   GR 826930–788932

Rough, nasty climb leads to sublime smooth grass cruise through Mallerstang and long gentle descent.

Melbecks Moor (Gunnerside & Melbecks Moor)   GR 946014–967985

A cruise of two halves, as the football manager would say. An eerie moonscape leads on to familiar grouse moor and sheep-grazed territory.

Whaw Moor (Langthwaite & Whaw Moor)   GR 975030–993015

You've climbed 300 metres to get here so enjoy the long gentle descent through mining spoils and heather scenery in a Big Country setting.

Moresdale Road (Langthwaite & Hurst Moor)   GR 027040–061035

With a prevailing westerly wind behind you on a sunny day you'll fly like a rocket with a grin on your face through rolling heather-clad hills

Over Harkerside Moor (Reeth & Harkerside Moor)   GR 044975–994956

You've sweated and grunted 320 metres up from the river, so relax as the wind blows you along this undulating balcony path. Great views over Swaledale

Castle Bolton towards Askrigg (Castle Bolton & Apedale)   GR 033918–954922

Cruise the northern slopes of Wensleydale over undulating stone tracks and smooth grass on one of the longest unbroken off-road stretches in the Dales

West Cam Road (Hawes, Dodd Fell & Burtersett)   GR 846872–830834

You're up close to 600m here so take oxygen as you cruise along parallel to the perfect U-shaped valley of Snaizeholme.

Stake Allotments (Bainbridge & Langstrothdale)   GR 937846–936817

High above Wensleydale, Raydale, Bishopdale and Wharfedale this is like the fabled North West Passage, the unknown link between settlements. Climb to a highpoint on Stake Moss and Hell Gap beckons...

Marrick Moor and Langthwaite (Marske to Arkengarthdale) GR 045997–031023

A near vertical climb up Fremington Edge suddenly stops and you're on the plateau of Marrick Moor with easy riding towards the big chimney, then west towards the fixed-grin descent to Storthwaite Hall.

Appendices

Tourist Information Offices

*Seasonal opening

Aysgarth Falls*   Tel: 01969 663424
aysgarth@ytbtic.co.uk

Hawes*   Tel: 01969 667450
hawes@ytbtic.co.uk

Horton in Ribblesdale   Tel: 01729 860333
horton@ytbtic.co.uk

Kirkby Stephen   Tel: 017683 71199
ks.tic@eden.gov.uk

Leyburn   Tel: 01969 623069
leyburn@ytbtic.co.uk

Reeth   Tel: 01748 884059
reeth@ytbtic.co.uk

Richmond   Tel: 01748 850252
richmond@ytbtic.co.uk

Sedbergh   Tel: 015396 20125
sedbergh@yorkshiredales.org.uk

Weather

www.bbc.co.uk/weather

www.metoffice.com

Food and Drink

Cafés

There are hundreds of cafes around, so we're just going to list a couple of faves. See the individual rides for more.

Pen-y-Ghent Café
Horton in Ribbleside   Tel: 01729 860333

Cross Keys
on the A683   Tel: 015396 20284

Ghyllfoot Café
Gunnerside   Tel: 01748 886239
March to October, closed Tuesdays

Pubs

Again, there are loads – there's pretty much one in every village. See the individual rides for recommendations. Here are a couple:

The New Inn
Appletreewick   Tel: 01756 720252

Tan Hill Inn – *The highest pub in England*
Tan Hill   Tel: 01833 628246

Red Lion
Langthwaite   Tel: 01748 884218

Kings Head
Gunnerside   Tel: 01748 886261

Accommodation

Youth Hostels

Visit www.yha.org.uk

Dentdale	Tel: 0870 770 5790
Grinton	Tel: 0870 770 5844
Hawes	Tel: 0870 770 5854
Keld	Tel: 0870 770 5888
Kettlewell	Tel: 0870 770 5896
Kirkby Stephen	Tel: 0870 770 5904

Hotels, Self Catering & B&B

Your best bet is to have a look on the websites listed later in this section, or to contact the Tourist Information Centre nearest to where you plan to ride.

Campsites

There are a few campsites dotted around the area. There are three near Hawes in Wensleydale. Swaledale has a couple near Keld and one near Muker and there is one near Langthwaite in Arkengarthdale.

Bike Shops

Hawes
Kudu Bikes
Also do bike hire   Tel: 01969 666088

Kirkby Stephen
Stephen McWhirter Cycles
Also do bike hire   Tel: 01768 371658

Richmond
Arthur Caygill Cycles   Tel: 01748 825469

There are loads more outside the Park boundary:

Kendal
Askew Cycles   Tel: 01539 728057
Brucie's Bikes   Tel: 01539 727230

Lancaster
The Edge Cycleworks   Tel: 01524 840800

Ripon
Moonglu   Tel: 01765 601106

Settle
The Station Yard   Tel: 01729 822216

Skipton
The Bicycle Shop   Tel: 01756 794386
Dave Ferguson Cycles
Also do bike hire   Tel: 01756 795367

Bike Hire

Fremington (near Reeth)
Dales Mountain Bike Hire
*Also organise courses, guiding &
mountain bike breaks*   Tel: 01748 884356

Castle Bolton
Wensleydale Bike Hire   Tel: 01969 623981

Dales Bike Liveries

The Yorkshire Dales is well on the way to becoming the first national park in Britain to establish a system of Bike Liveries across its region. The plan is for fully equipped bike liveries to be located at various MTB-friendly pubs and cafés throughout the region and will offer riders secure bike storage, workshops, hoses and so on.

Modelled on John Pitcher's awesome facility behind the **New Inn** in Appletreewick, liveries will be established in key areas of the park, such as Settle, Hawes and Reeth.

Baggage handling will be offered between liveries, making point-to-point multi-day rides across the Dales a real option. Guiding services will also be available.

Contact the **YDNPA** or **John Pitcher** for more information.

Other Publications & Websites

Yorkshire Dales Mountain Biking – The South Dales
Nick Cotton, Vertebrate Graphics

Off-Road Trails & Quiet Lanes
Keith Bradbury, Vertebrate Graphics

Where to Mountain Bike in Britain
Nicky Crowther, Open Air Books

www.v-graphics.co.uk/publications

www.yorkshiredales.org.uk

www.yorkshire-dales.com

www.mtbthedales.org.uk

The Author
Nick Cotton

Nick Cotton has written over 30 bike guides in the last 12 years, riding more than 20,000 miles all over Britain during the course of his research. He has travelled and trekked extensively, climbing to over 18,000ft on three continents and has cycled in Morocco and Patagonia (the worst winds in the world!).

He lives in the Lune Valley in Cumbria, between the Lakes and the Dales. He is very partial to fine coffee, real ale and cakes, especially on the course of a ride. Six feet four and 14 stones needs a lot of fuel.

The photographer
Andy Heading

Despite regular trips *oop north* over the years (mainly for Polaris and Trailquest events), Andy's lasting memory of the Dales was getting two 'volunteers' to dress up as Wallace and Gromit for a cheesy Wensleydale photo-feature. Since photographing this guide, he's realised there's much more to Yorkshire than cursing and were-rabbits, and looks forward to biking there again soon. In the meantime, he is the official photographer to the European Athletic Association, and lives in a cheese-free zone in Matlock, Derbyshire.

Vertebrate Graphics

Vertebrate Graphics Ltd is a full service graphic design agency, specialising in print design, web development and publishing. We design a wide range of communication material from wedding stationery to corporate brochures.

As well as being one of the largest agencies in the UK to work within the outdoor leisure sector, our experienced team of designers produce work for IT companies, educational organisations, including colleges and universities, financial institutions and the retail sector.

Vertebrate Graphics has had substantial success in the design and production of specialist outdoor books. These include **Hillwalking – The Official Handbook of the Mountain Leader and Walking Group Leader Schemes** (a best-selling outdoor title for three years running), and two highly praised guidebooks for rock climbers – the award-winning **Lake District Rock – Selected Rock Climbs in The Lake District** and **The Roaches – Staffordshire Grit**.

For more information please refer to our website at **www.v-graphics.co.uk**, or contact us direct at **info@v-graphics.co.uk**.

Order form for
VG Vertebrate Graphics
PUBLICATIONS & CD-ROMS

Item	Qty	Price
hill & trail **walking** » books		(inc P&P)
Day Walks in the Peak District		£12.95
mountain **biking** » books & cd-roms		
Off-Road Trails & Quiet Lanes		£12.95
Yorks Dales – North MTB Book		£15.95
Yorks Dales – North CD-ROM		£7.50
Yorks Dales – North Book & CD-ROM Bundle		£15.95
Yorks Dales – South MTB Book		£15.95
Yorks Dales – South CD-ROM		£7.50
Yorks Dales – South Book & CD-ROM Bundle		£21.00
White Peak MTB Book		£14.95
White Peak CD-ROM		£7.50
White Peak Book & CD-ROM Bundle		£20.00
Dark Peak MTB Book		£14.95
Dark Peak CD-ROM		£7.50
Dark Peak Book & CD-ROM Bundle		£20.00
South West MTB Book		£14.95
South West CD-ROM		£7.50
South West Book & CD-ROM Bundle		£20.00
other » books		
Getting to Grips with GPS		£14.95
	TOTAL £	

Fill in this coupon and send it along with a cheque to:

Vertebrate Graphics,
Crescent House, 228 Psalter Lane, Sheffield SII 8UT
Make cheques payable to **Vertebrate Graphics Ltd**.
Credit card payments are accepted at our website. Orders dispatched by return.

Name: ....

Address: ....

....

Postcode: ....

E-mail: ....

☐ **Vertebrate Graphics** will *never* pass on your details to third parties, but if you do not want to receive information on future VG Hill Walking, Mountain Biking or Climbing and Bouldering Guides, please tick here.

You can also place your order @ www.**v-graphics**.co.uk/publications